CONCILIUM

THEOLOGY IN THE AGE OF RENEWAL

CONCILIUM

CONCILIUM/VOL. 29

SPIRITUALITY

OPPORTUNITIES FOR BELIEF AND BEHAVIOR

edited by CHRISTIAN DUQUOC, O.P.

VOLUME 29

CONCILIUM
theology in the age of renewal

PAULIST PRESS
NEW YORK, N.Y./ GLEN ROCK, N.J.

Copyright © 1967 by
Paulist Fathers, Inc. and *Stichting Concilium*

All Rights Reserved
Nothing contained in this publication shall be duplicated and/or made
public by means of print, photography, microfilm, or in any other manner,
without the previous consent of *Paulist Press* and *Stichting Concilium*.

Library of Congress Catalog Card Number: 67–31523

Suggested Decimal Classification: 291.4

Paulist Press assumes responsibility for the accuracy of the English trans-
lations in this Volume.

PAULIST PRESS
EXECUTIVE OFFICES: 304 W. 58th Street, New York, N.Y. and 21 Harris-
town Road, Glen Rock, N.J.
Executive Publisher: John A. Carr, C.S.P.
Executive Manager: Alvin A. Illig, C.S.P.
Asst. Executive Manager: Thomas E. Comber, C.S.P.

EDITORIAL OFFICES: 304 W. 58th Street, New York, N.Y.
Editor: Kevin A. Lynch, C.S.P.
Managing Editor: Urban P. Intondi

Printed and bound in the United States of America by
The Colonial Press Inc., Clinton, Mass.

CONTENTS

PART II

BIBLIOGRAPHICAL SURVEY

PART III

DOCUMENTATION CONCILIUM
Office of the Executive Secretary
Nijmegen, Netherlands

PREFACE

Christian Duquoc, O.P. /Lyons, France

The reader may be surprised to find pages devoted to racism, the war in Vietnam and underdevelopment in a volume dealing with spirituality. Some may be shocked. For them the pursuit of God and the universal love of man have nothing to do with politics. Because of the reservations that will probably be made, I would have liked to have included an article dealing with the question whether Christian love implies a political aspect or not. This article was commissioned but unfortunately not written. This failure was due to circumstances beyond our control. Nevertheless it is symbolic, as is clear from what I read recently in a theological article: "Charity does not calculate; it inspires all things but prescribes nothing, and that is why it creates a new world; it presupposes an absence of judgments and particular forms which would limit the universality of its end; at the level of what is finite it constitutes the privileged experience of what is pure action, absolute love."

But what is such a pure action or such an absolute love in this world if not a mere abstraction? Spiritual authors have tried hard to eliminate competition between the love of God and brotherly love. They were afraid of depriving God of what was given to others. For this they refer to the experience of militant Christians who fall into activism and forget God, and occasionally proceed to swell the ranks of Marxism. I do not think that this

1

abandonment of religion is caused by some kind of competition. It is rooted in that void of the very charity which is ennobled by the attribute of universality. This void encourages atheism: by denying the mediating role of concrete life it substitutes sacramental actions.

If I celebrate fraternal love at the eucharistic meal and refuse to translate its meaning into concrete life, I either mock God or God alienates himself from me by allowing me to live in imagination what is never lived in fact. Charity therefore refers to the particular experience of love whatever friendly or political means it uses. Universality is not an empty frame but the aspect of a genuine particular experience, or, ultimately, a Christian experience. If the Churches fail to show forth this link in the concrete challenges created by the world of actuality, they simply take refuge in verbalism and show that God, in contrast to him to whom the prophets of Israel bore witness, has turned away from our daily existence.

In spite of its chaotic appearance, only one purpose runs through this volume, that of demythologizing certain tenacious prejudices that turn Christianity into a mere abstraction or pious exhortation.

PART I
ARTICLES

Jean-Yves Jolif, O.P./*Eveux, France*

The Real Challenge of Atheistic Humanism

Within the past century and a half, a striking shift in outlook has taken place. To the Christian thinker it is a shocking and scandalous thing. A new humanism has been formulated on the theoretical and practical level, and it has taken a startling turn.

Earlier Humanism

An earlier brand of humanism attacked the Christian faith and criticized its faults, showing its inconsistencies and absurdities on the rational plane. This earlier brand of humanism was something to which the believer had gradually adjusted. He had a stockpile of arguments that enabled him to confront this humanism with a certain measure of confidence, even when he was not able to convince his adversary.

When we examine the religious literature of the early 19th century, we find that contemporary apologists had learned how to confront the philosophy of the Enlightenment. They were able to turn the philosophers' arguments to their own advantage and to hold their own against their intellectual adversaries. The writings of their philosophical opponents became a source of ammunition for the apologists' defense of religion. At that stage in history, religion was still able to vindicate its superiority over atheism, to show that it alone could fully satisfy man's interests.

Man did not lose anything by being religious; on the contrary, religion was the only thing that guaranteed self-fulfillment.

A New Challenge

The whole problem takes on new dimensions when Christianity runs up against a new brand of humanism in the second half of the 19th century. From that point on, Christian revelation is no longer rejected out of hand. Its tenets are no longer regarded as deviations from sound reasoning. Instead, the meaning of Christian revelation is acknowledged to be a sound, human aspiration, one which must be supported and turned into a reality. Christianity is now regarded as an authentic platform, insofar as it envisions unity among men and brotherly love.

But now the atheistic critic sets out to prove that this platform can only be realized if Christianity itself is eliminated. So long as the quest for universal love is directed by religion, it is doomed to the realm of abstract ideals; it is no more than a hope that cannot be realized in concrete reality. The duty of humanism now is to promote and realize in history the human aspirations that Christianity proclaimed but could not bring about.

Seen in this light, humanism is Christianity's closest relative —and her most radical adversary. On the one hand, it seeks to achieve the same goal that was envisioned by Christianity, even though the goal was not clearly spelled out by the latter. On the other hand, it presupposes that this goal can only be realized in a process that will have nothing to do with religion. This new humanism is convinced of one thing: Christianity is radically incapable of effectively realizing human ideals; it is, in the strict sense of the word, *inhuman.*

The Christian's Quandary

Now this type of criticism was most disconcerting to the Christian believer. To the extent that he really understood his faith, he felt justified in believing that he was called to a life of reconciliation. Through Christ he was to reconcile himself with Christ and with other men. His relationship with God did not detach him from the world and project him into some foreign realm; instead, it introduced him into the fullness of life, which was a *truly human* brand of life and a means of self-fulfillment even though it was a gratuitous gift from God. Moreover, this new life was presented as one of total love. How could such a life be interpreted as one of self-destruction? How could it be regarded as inhuman? Was it not a serious mistake to believe that atheism is the only way to achieve a life that the believer concretely experiences?

The Problem of Atheism

Any believer who is familiar with the problem just posed is tempted to misunderstand its implications. As a believer, he is inclined to feel that the game is fixed and is being played with loaded dice. But it is to his own advantage to avoid jumping to such conclusions. They tend to make him overlook important aspects of the problem, to hide questions that must be answered and to miss the real issues posed by atheism.

The Church's Historical Shortcomings

Some are inclined, for example, to explain atheism as a re-action to the Church of the 19th century; but this explanation is inadequate.

There is no doubt, of course, that 19th-century Christianity weighed heavily in the debate, and that it gave people much reason to regard Christianity as an anti-human force, one which precluded the establishment of interpersonal relations.

The 19th-century Church was a clerical Church which treated the laity as irresponsible children. It gave little indication that its salvific message had any real contact with the lives of men. It expressed distrust and even condemnation of progress, science, liberty, democracy and justice—all the forces which that epoch had come to recognize as basic values and urgent necessities. Is it any wonder that people regarded the kingdom of God—prefigured and represented by the Church—as the negation of the most important values of man.

To the exploited worker the Church held out the promise of a future life, the value of suffering and the transiency of earthly life. It seemed to distract the unfortunate from their real problems and to confirm their miserable lot.

That is how atheism saw the contemporary Church and the message it seemed to represent. It is worth noting that some religious individuals, who refused to be classed as atheists, also moved away from Christianity. They saw it tied up with a contemptuous outlook on man, incapable of assimilating and bolstering the new enthusiasm that mankind was bringing to its task in history. To a large extent, this was the attitude of the French workers in the second half of the 19th century. The workers abandoned the Church because they felt that Christianity had deceived them. It did not appreciate the nobility of work, nor the grandeur of the social struggle. Far from being irreligious, the workers were looking for a new religion, one which would understand them and take part in their passionate struggle for genuine brotherhood and a more human society.

One cannot deny that Christianity's shortcomings, as an historical reality, did much to stimulate interest in atheism. People looked to atheism for the means to turn the vague promises of faith into concrete realities, for faith seemed unable to do this of itself. But it would be a mistake to regard this as the complete explanation, for atheism is more than a simple reaction to a particular manifestation of Christianity at a given point in history.

An Inadequate Approach

Such an explanation might well give rise to excessive optimism and overconfidence. The believer might expect a process of *aggiornamento* to solve the whole problem with a wave of the hand. If we fail to realize the depth of atheism's challenge to the faith, we shall not be able to define exactly what an updating should accomplish, or to isolate the area in which the believer could give revitalized expression to his faith. Most important of all, we would find it hard to avoid remaining prisoners of an outlook and an approach that atheistic humanism has rendered obsolete.

Let me stress this point once again. If a person tries to explain atheism solely as a reaction to a particular historical manifestation of Christianity, if he suggests that only this particular brand of Christianity is hurt by the atheist's criticism, then he is not really contributing anything to the debate. In fact, he is succumbing to a way of thinking which, in the atheist's opinion, is the surest proof that Christianity, of its very nature, is incapable of realizing the goals it envisions. It only serves to convince the atheist that a breakthrough to achievement must involve a breakup with Christianity.

What a person is really doing in this case is trying to distinguish the *essence* of Christianity from a particular historical manifestation of it. By carefully distinguishing between the two, he hopes to show that condemnation of the latter does not affect the former at all. But in so doing, he is creating a break between the two. In saying that Christianity's shape in history is distinct from its essence, he is implying that the Christian ideal never shows up as an objective historical reality, that its historical shape contradicts and deforms its ideals. He thus sets up a chasm between the external and the internal, between aspiration and accomplishment, between man's interior life and his outward behavior. To escape the critic's lash, he appeals to an intangible interior world. His attempted defense actually lends credence to the viewpoint of the atheist and bolsters it. Why is this?

The Atheist's Complaint

Atheistic humanism does not reject Christianity solely on account of its historical shortcomings. The data of past history is not the only basis for the atheist's position. He is not to be identified with the disillusioned Christian who abandons the Church because it has failed him.

As the atheist sees it, the most important point is not that Christianity has displayed shortcomings in history; the important point is that the Christian faith is incapable of concretely realizing and actualizing the ideals and goals it proclaims. Its inability is brought out all the more by its appeal to a hidden essence that is lived in the interior of one's being. By appealing to this inner life, Christianity succumbs to delusion and proclaims its own ineffectiveness.

The atheist feels, first of all, that the search for some essence above and beyond historical reality is an illusory quest; it is chasing after shadows. For there is no reality except that to be found in the web of relations between man and nature, man and things, and man and man. The first tenet of atheistic humanism is based on the principle that man is not an idea, that he cannot be separated from actual events, that he *is* the concrete datum in a certain sense. If man emits an aura of transcendence, if his presence inevitably leads us beyond tangible realities, this thrust is not a speculative movement toward some abstract essence; it is instead a practical activity in the real world. When we speak of man, we are not speaking about a subsistent spiritual principle unrelated to other men and other beings; we are talking about a potential reservoir of activity, capable of turning reality upside down and bringing unsuspected meanings to light.

For this reason the believer is on the wrong track when he tries to refute the atheist by appealing to some abstract essence. Christianity is not and cannot be this hidden essence, existing somewhere beyond the data of reality. Christianity is actually this form which concrete existence takes, this particular way of relating to other men and other beings, this concrete and visible behavior pattern, this truly historical reality which is perceived by the senses. These are the only true realities embodied in the term "Christianity". When the believer refuses to link Christianity with objective reality, when he looks for some so-called deeper reality, he is an idealist living in a world of abstractions.

In such a case he can never turn his vaunted ideals and claims into concrete realities. He may talk about universal love and dream about the reconciliation of all men; but his concrete life in history will contrast sharply with these ideals. If his ideals are achieved in some subjective state or some after-life, he could not find any field of practical experience in which to realize them. If the essence of Christianity is verified in the subjective interior of the believer, it could not be pictured as a project to be realized in concrete history. The relationship between the believer and the world of faith is a contemplative, speculative relationship.

To put it another way: the world of Christian values is not to be found in a process that opens man to the secular world; it is found in a process of interiorization, in plumbing the depths of one's own subjectivity. In short, the believer is imprisoned in a process of abstraction because he lives in an unreal world of *faits accomplis*. The believer loses himself in a world of shadows; he cannot see the real world, where nothing can be taken for granted, where everything must be achieved by practical action.

Christianity's Dilemma

In the eyes of the atheist, this is the fundamental error of the Christian faith. The believer is justified in refusing to equate Christianity with a particular manifestation of it in history, in claiming that it involves *something more* than its visible characteristics. But he is mistaken in equating this *more* with some essence that is above and beyond history and compromised by it. The *more* in Christianity is a possibility for practical action, the need for active work that is truly capable of transforming relations between men.

But, says the atheist, the process of interiorization is an essential one for the Christian faith. However much Christianity may talk about building concrete relations between human beings, it has never given any evidence that it takes this task seriously. As a matter of fact, it could not do so without denying its own nature. It would have to reverse itself completely, giving up its emphasis on the interior life and focusing on the concrete realities of human existence, on objective facts and the visible world—the only place where man is to be found.

Man, says the atheist, is not an abstract idea. He *is* the world in which he exists. He is the one who gives shape to other beings as soon as he makes contact with them.

The Thrust of Atheistic Humanism

If our remarks are accurate, then we can say that the problem posed by atheistic humanism is not solely, or even primarily, a speculative question; it is in the practical order. The central question is whether Christianity is in fact doomed to the realm of the abstract and the unhistorical, or whether it is truly meant to transform history (even though it is not to be equated with this work of transformation).

Another characteristic of contemporary atheism is also evident. In criticizing Christianity, it is dominated by the desire to get away from the shadowy world of unreality, to find the realm where man truly does exist.

Atheism's rejection of the "other world" and the "interior life" is only the negative side of its program. From there it moves on to explore concrete existence. At this point Nietzsche's attack on Platonic metaphysics joins forces with Marx's materialism.

The atheist asserts that reality is actually what had always been regarded as fleeting appearances. He stubbornly insists that man is not the reflective spirit described by philosophy from time immemorial. Man *is* the world of men, the whole web of institutions and relationships to be found in the sensible world. In laying hold of this world we are not laying hold of shadowy appearances. Or, to put it another way, these appearances are not deceitful images hiding the real from us. They are the evidence of the real; and if there is something beyond these appearances, it must be discernible in them.

In the eyes of the atheist this reversal of the classic philosophical approach is the only way to move beyond solipsism once and for all. It is the only way in which human relations become possible. If man is the subjective reality described by Descartes, how can there be any interpersonal relations? I could verify my own reality, of course, but how could I verify the reality of other human spirits? The only way I encounter them is in objective, external situations. When I see men passing outside my window, I have only the evidence of my senses to vouch for their existence. Knowledge of other men becomes an inexplicable mystery in a Cartesian framework.

But now suppose man really is the reality we encounter through our senses. Suppose he really is the concrete web of relationships we experience in the world. Then there is no mystery as to how we come to know others. Other men are an immediate datum of experience, and I come to know them in the very same process by which I come to know myself. In defining myself as a sensible, material, historical being, I move beyond the confining limits of my own individuality. I become accessible to others and they to me.

Thus, to the extent that atheistic humanism represents an attempt to peg man as an objective being, it is essentially a desire to establish a real link between human beings. It is a passionate attempt to create a web of concrete relationships that will enable each individual to grasp the reality of man through his encounter with other men.

Henri-Marie Féret, O.P./*Paris, France*

Brotherly Love in the Church as the Sign of the Kingdom

This theme implies that there are certain tensions within the Christian's experience of charity. These tensions have always existed. But the theologian who studies the unfolding of God's plan in human history will recognize that these tensions are expressed today in ways that are mostly new. In the light of that "concrete and historical" theology which was discussed by Pope Paul and Prof. Skydsgaard on October 17, 1963, they appear, with the whole question of brotherly love, as linked by right and in fact with the new duties of the Christian in the present historical encounter between the Church and the world since the Council.

I

THE PRELIMINARY POINTS

1. *Brotherly Love and the Love of God*

In order to avoid all misunderstanding, let us first get rid of that alleged tension which, according to some spiritual authors, exists between the love of brother and the love of God. Apart from the fact that it has nothing special to contribute to today's problems, this false tension has too often been put forward as a problem of Christian life in writings that have unduly been given

15

the status of theological treatises. These writings, or rather the
spiritual experiences they convey, show in fact far more that these
two kinds of love are inseparable than that there is a pseudo-
tension between them, even taking for granted that these experiences are valid. The follower of the Christ of the gospels knows
by experience that he can no more love his brother without loving the Father than he can love the Father without loving the
brother. The more he advances in Christian life, the better he
realizes that the oneness of this twofold and unique love is basically, in concrete psychology, an inward and active disposition
toward communion with the other, a communion in which, ultimately, the beatitude of the poor in spirit (which is related to the
Father) is identical with the beatitude of the meek (related to the
neighbor (cf. Mt. 5, 3-4 and Lk. 6, 20).

The reason for this progressive unity of love lies in the fact
that the authentic love of the Gospel is a love of communion and
of friendship.[1] In this experience and this search for communion
not only is there no opposition between the brotherly relations
with people and the filial relation with the Father but we also
find in the mystery of the Son the transcendent foundation of
these two relationships, and in the mystery of the Spirit the
equally transcendent foundation for deepening and universalizing
these relationships. Through Jesus, at the same time the true
Adam and the Son of the living God, we are brothers (1 Cor.
1, 9). In the Spirit, himself God's mystery of an infinite communion of love between distinct Persons, we can and must grow
in this search for, and this experience of, communion in friendship which is, in concrete terms, the practice of brotherly love.
These are traditionally accepted certainties, and the Council
had only to remind us of them in general terms without having

---

[1] The understanding of charity as friendship, and therefore first of all
as the pursuit of friendship, is more than ever necessary for Christians
in the practice of the precept of love toward all men. I have spoken about
this in *Charité et vérité* (Paris/Lyon, 1950), pp. 53-106 and "Pour une
Eglise des Béatitudes de la pauvreté," in *L'Eglise des pauvres* (Paris,
1965), pp. 237f.

to discuss them again.² If, on the other hand, the conciliar
documents urge us to look at certain, partly new, consequences
of these traditional data, the reason is that what is new is the
present situation in the relationship of Church and world.

2. *The Primacy in Practice of Brotherly Love*

In order to deal with the new demands created by this new situation in matters of love, this first point must be followed by two
equally important demands. The first concerns the exact nature
of the concrete relations between the love of God and love of
brother. All New Testament scholars agree that in practically
all the relevant texts the expression "love of God" must be understood as a genitive of subject, not of object;³ in other words, not
as the love we have toward God (object) but on the contrary
God's (subject) love toward us, the love that he has commanded
us to spread to the brother through the Spirit. The first Epistle of
John explains this extensively (1 Jn. 4, 7-12).

² In the *Constitution on the Church* (n. 4), the Church "is in some
way the sacrament, i.e., at the same time the sign and the means of
intimate union with God and of the unity of all mankind". Section 40
quotes Mark 12, 30 and John 13, 34 and recalls that the perfection of
Christian life is none other than the perfection of the twofold and yet
single charity. Section 42 states: "It is the charity toward God and
neighbor which marks the true disciple of Christ." In nn. 49 and 50
this charity is said to constitute the unity between the Church in
heaven and the Church on earth. In the *Decree on Ecumenism* (nn.
1; 2, par. 2) it is the Spirit who, through love, is the principle of the
Church's unity. "For the faithful can achieve depth and ease in strength-
ening mutual brotherhood to the degree that they enjoy profound communion with the Father, the Word, and the Spirit" (n. 7). The *Decree
on Religious Life* (n. 8, par. 2) states that the two dimensions of the
one love cannot be separated. The *Constitution on the Church in the
Modern World* (n. 21, par. 5) teaches that brotherly love is the revelation of God and in n. 24 (par. 2 and 3) that it cannot be separated
from the love of God. This point is the main theme of chapter II
of the second part of this Constitution. See also nn. 38, par. 1 and 57,
par. 2, etc.

³ For the statistics of the verb and its derivatives in the New Testament,
see C. Spicq, *Agapè dans le Nouveau Testament* (Paris, 1958), Vol. I,
p. 9. For the Synoptics, *ibid.* pp. 156ff. and 173; for Paul, *ibid.* pp.
303ff. and Vol. I (1959), pp. 302ff.; for Peter and Jude, Vol. II, pp.
359ff. and for the Johannine writings, Vol. III (1959), pp. 313ff.

With this evidence from the New Testament in mind, we should realize that a distinction, implying priority, between love of God and love of neighbor, which is only valid at the level of juridical statements or of formal theology, has too often and unduly been applied to the level of Christian experience in practice. This led to a twofold danger. It either encouraged a religion of evasion under the pretext of loving God first, or reduced the real theological value of brotherly love. As a juridical statement of "precepts" it is of course true that loving God "with one's whole heart, one's whole soul, one's whole mind" is distinct from loving one's brother, and it is superior to it in the sense that the absolute is distinct from, and superior to, the relative. On the other hand, it is no less true that in actual experience the love of brother not only cannot be separated from the love of God but has, with regard to this love of God, a genuine priority in practice and origin. Only through loving our brother can we love God. St. Matthew (5, 23-24), St. Mark 11, 25), St. Luke (6, 46, following on the parable about the mote in the brother's eye) and St. John (1 Jn. 2, 3-11; 3, 14-24; 4, 7-13; 4, 19-21), to quote only a few, are all agreed on this point. They are followed by St. Augustine and St. Thomas who say the same thing and the reason they adduce is the same for them as for the whole New Testament: that presence and action of the Spirit, which I shall speak of.

Augustine said: "The love of God is first in the order of precepts, but the love of brother is the first in the order of action . . . Love, therefore, your neighbor and look into yourself to see where his love of neighbor comes from. There you will see God as far as you are capable of it. Begin, therefore, by loving your neighbor, share your bread with the hungry, open your house to the roofless, clothe the naked and despise no one of. the same human race. When you have done all this, what will be your reward? Like the sun in the morning, your light will rise (cf. Is. 68, 7-8), and your light is your God himself . . ." [4]

[4] St. Augustine, *Tract. XVII in Io. Ev.* (*P.L.* 35, c.1531). See also nn. 9-11. In n. 10, for instance, he says: "When you love your neighbor

St. Thomas wrote: "In the order of perfection and dignity
. . . love of God comes first before love of neighbor. But in
the order of origin and disposition love of neighbor precedes the
love of God insofar as the act is concerned." [5] Speculative theology, therefore, even in the strictest sense accepts this priority
of the genesis of love of neighbor over love of God which runs
throughout the New Testament, and this priority implies a priority in practical training and experience. Love of the other is
therefore the necessary embodiment of the very experience of
love of God.

3. *Brotherly Love and the Mission of the Spirit in the People
   of God*

From the point of view of concrete and historical theology
this point assumes still greater importance, and so we reach the
third certainty which I take as generally accepted and which
will inspire the rest of this analysis of what brotherly love demands of us today.

In the perspective of the concrete unfolding of God's plan in
human history this certainty concerns the fact that, if brotherly
love is the fullness of the law (cf. Gal. 5, 14; 6, 2; Rom. 13,
8-10), if it is the typical commandment of the definitive kingdom of God in the new and eternal covenant (cf. Mt. 7, 12;
Jn. 13, 34), this is because, at the end and at the peak of this
divine dispensation, it is linked with the full communication
of the transcendent mystery of the God who is love, in the
Spirit, to the People of God. Just as the mission of the Word
in Jesus the Messiah makes us walk in the light through faith

---

and care for him, you are on the right path. Where will this path lead
you, if not to the Lord God, to him whom we must love with all our
heart, all our soul and all our mind?" There are also fine passages in
Tract. VI in I^{am} Ep. Ioannis, ch. 3 such as: "By what shall everyone
know that he has received the Spirit? Let him listen to his own heart: if
he loves the brother, the Spirit of God dwells in him." And again in
his *De Trinitate* 8, 8 (*P.L.* 42, c.558ff.): "When we love the brother
with true love, we love the brother through God, and it is impossible not
to love above all that very love by which we love the brother."

[5] *Ia IIae, q. 68, a. 8, ad 2.*

in Jesus because God himself is light, so the mission of the Spirit makes us walk in love through the love of brother because God himself is love. Here we recognize the two themes of the first Epistle of St. John, which makes it also clear that these two divine missions do not only run parallel but are closely interdependent. For the People of God in the historical phase of the Church, the final phase of salvation history, it is therefore the Spirit who has become the first law of the spiritual life of the members in matters of both love and freedom.[6] Now the essence of the mystery of the Spirit is precisely that it is a mystery of communion and unity in love.[7] It is in this perspective, above all, that we must see that new and deeper development of brotherly love, demanded by our modern society, if it is to be the sign of this presence of God at the very heart of human life.[8]

II

THE PRESENT SITUATION AND BROTHERLY LOVE

Having tried to eliminate the main possible misunderstandings, we can now turn to this new historical situation which seems to impose new demands on Christian charity while also creating some new difficulties and tensions.

1. *A Minority Church in a Unified World*

At present, human history is dominated by the plain and irreversible fact that the world has become one whatever crises may still beset man before the unity has been achieved completely. The present process of socialization expresses, and at

[6] Cf. I. de la Potterie and S. Lyonnet, *La vie selon l'Esprit condition du chrétien* (Paris, 1965).

[7] "Peuple de Dieu, mystère de charité," in *Vie spirituelle* (Oct., 1945), pp. 242-62.

[8] *Constitution on the Church in the Modern World*, n. 22, par. 4: "The Christian man, conformed to the likeness of that Son who is the first-born of many brothers, receives 'the firstfruits of the Spirit' (Rom. 8, 23) by which he becomes capable of discharging the new law of love (Rom. 8, 1-11)." Cf. *Constitution on the Church*, nn. 4, 7, 13, 39; and *Decree on Ecumenism*, n. 2.

the same time imposes, this new dimension on man's existence in every field, economic, social, national, international, cultural and even religious. All in all, the solidarity of all men is now proceeding at a planetary scale.

At the same time the various collective units, whether social, national or international, and even the Church itself, are forced to be more aware of, and realistic about, the very great diversity of the spiritual groups that compose this humanity in process of unification and increasing interdependence. The geographically limited, coherent but also often confused systems of combining the spiritual and the temporal which marked Byzantine and Slavonic Christianity in the East, where they are paradoxically projected into the totalitarianism and militant atheism of some Marxist States, or Latin Christianity in the West, where Catholicism or a form of Protestantism is still the established religion of some States, begin to disappear. Some may already foresee in this the last convulsions of the beast of the Apocalypse in the light of the eschatological warnings of the Book of Revelation, which find here their proper background.[9] Yet, the world progresses toward collective systems which in fact as well as in their constitutions recognize the distinction between what is God's and what is Caesar's as taught by Jesus and which recognize religious freedom at least in principle. It is this historical context which gives meaning to the *Declaration on Religious Freedom* and makes it providentially relevant.

These first very general indications of the present situation make us already sense that Christian charity can no longer be limited to the domestic scope of the various individual Christian bodies as various in-groups spread about in time and space, but must now extend to humanity as a whole with its universal dimensions embracing an extreme diversity of even mutually opposed groups, all closely interconnected. It becomes, therefore, inevitable that within these groups the monolithic and gregarious mentality will yield to extremely varied currents of

[9] Cf. *L'Apocalypse de s. Jean, vision chrétienne de l'histoire* (Paris, 1943), pp. 199f. and 283f.

ideas (cf. 1 Tim. 4, 1ff.; 2 Tim. 4, 3ff.). If, in the light of the
New Testament, we can therefore expect difficult times for the
Church (cf. Mt. 7, 15ff.; 24, 4-5 and paral. pass.; 2 Pet. 2, 1ff.;
Rev. 13, 11ff., etc.), one can see also, and more positively, that
this will lead ultimately to the indivisibility of the universal communion of saints and the full personal value of every human
vocation.

This is not all, however. The findings of demography related
to the growth of humanity on the one hand and to that of the
Christian Churches or Confessions on the other, show that the
Church is already and will become increasingly a minority in
this world, even if we think of the Church in the light of the
Decree on Ecumenism. At the same time the Church will become increasingly aware of the mission Christ charged her with,
to be present "among the nations to the confines of the earth"
and "to preach the Good News to all creatures" (Acts 1, 8; Mt.
28, 18; Mk. 16, 15, etc.) and this awareness is growing geographically, sociologically and spiritually. At a time, therefore,
when their love of brother must be the sign of God's coming in
a world which is becoming both more universalist and pluralist
at every level, Christians are also forced to realize that they are
becoming a minority among men. Thus the wider and more
complex the world becomes for the scope of their witness, the
more the actual scope of their ecclesiastical life will shrink and
become no doubt more difficult for many of them. Yet, they
will always be more in need of this life in order to feed their
witness.

2. *Cohesion in the Church and Universality of Love*

Close cohesion among Christians and the universal responsibility implied in brotherly love have always been interrelated.
Therefore there has also always been a certain tension in the
exercise of charity between the concern to maintain this "be-
longing to the Church" and the concern with a total missionary
presence in the world. The clear statement in the fourth gospel:
"By this *all* men will know that you are my disciples, if you

have love for one another" (Jn. 13, 35), has always been understood in that universal sense which marks so many of the teachings of Jesus. It is very clear in the parable (Lk. 10, 25-37) where it is a Samaritan, therefore a brother who was an "enemy", a heretic and an idolater, who is held up to the legal specialist as an example of the Christian attitude toward others.

While this most universal love was demanded of the followers of Jesus, other texts of the New Testament, and particularly the ecclesiology developed in the Acts of the Apostles, taught that an effective and missionary practice of charity (cf. Acts 2, 47; 4, 33; etc.) could only belong to believers who were actively involved in the specific activities of their ecclesial community. Luke enumerates four characteristics of the original community of Jesus' disciples: "the teaching of the apostles, life in common, the breaking of the bread and prayer" (Acts 2, 42), and the two last ones concern the messianic value of the priesthood. These characteristics recalled, for both the life of grace and the ministerial functions, the importance of full participation in the three constitutive elements of the messianic Church, the prophecy, kingship and priesthood of Jesus the Messiah and Son of the living God. Only a Church that is the prophetic community of faith in the incarnate Word, the priestly community of redemption and perfect spiritual worship and the kingly community of the love of the Spirit—that Church with her ministry founded on Peter's confession (Mt. 16, 16-18)[10] and her nature founded on the mystery of the God-Man Jesus (Acts 11; 1 Cor. 3, 11f.; Rom. 9, 32-33) can gather all mankind through the charity of her members into the mystery of the true Adam. In him they are all brothers through the one and only fatherhood of the transcendent God (Mt. 23, 9; Lk. 1, 26-28 and 3, 23-38; 1 Cor. 15, 45; Gal. 4, 4-6; Rom. 5, 14; Jn. 1, 12-13). Through him they are taken up in the mystery of the communion

---

[10] According to Augustine it is for, and because of, his confession of faith in Jesus as the Messiah and Son of God that Peter became the rock. Cf. A. M. La Bonnardière, "Tu es Petrus. La péricope Matthieu 16, 13-23 dans l'oeuvre de s. Augustin," in *Irénikon* (1961), pp. 450-99.

of love which is the Spirit sent by Jesus to his Church (2 Cor. 13, 13; Rom. 5, 5; etc.).

Thus, the participation in that life which is both supernatural (mission of the Son and mission of the Spirit) and institutional (the three apostolic functions that correspond to the three messianic aspects of the Church) dominated from the beginning the necessary missionary and eschatological unfolding of brotherly love, the specific commandment of the Lord. This was true for the first community of Jerusalem, for the community of Antioch from which Paul set out on his mission (Acts 11, 26; 13, 2-3), and will remain true for the Church throughout the ages.

While it is true that this tension between the Church's life and the openness of a brotherly love that must effectively witness to God's presence among all men belongs to all ages, it will nevertheless assume different forms and facets according to the particular phase in the unfolding of salvation history. In the present situation we have already begun to realize that, on the one hand, Christian brotherly love will only be able to be this effective witness if it becomes more universal, more supple, more "eschatological", than ever before, while on the other hand the minority situation of the Church will make it no doubt more difficult to maintain a real authenticity and cohesion in that ecclesial life that Christians will stand more than ever in need of.

3. *Brotherly Love as the Sign of Messianic Deliverance and Eschatological Judgment*

There is another tension which is inherent in the Christian experience of brotherly love. According to the Scriptures the coming of God inseparably unites the coming-to-save, which is already fulfilled in Jesus and is the perfect fulfillment of the law of charity as set out in the Sermon on the Mount (Mt. 5, 17—7, 12), with the eschatological coming-in-judgment, of which no one knows the day or hour but of which the believer knows that man will be judged precisely by the way he has practiced this brotherly love in all its aspects and which is the "constitution" of God's kingdom, prepared from the beginning according to the eschatological discourse of Matthew 25, 31-46. The "last days" are therefore at the same time salvation and judgment; ultimately, it is the practice or the blasphemous refusal of this brotherly love in which God's own love offers itself to man, that will decide whether man will enter into the plan of God's salvation or whether he will judge and condemn himself. As the sign of God's coming-to-save ("By this all will know", etc., Jn. 13, 55) brotherly love already bestows beatitude on those who accept. But this brotherly love is also the anticipating sign of the eschatological judgment, not only for believers who can recognize its constantly increasing demands, but also for non-believers to whom it reveals the advances of the God of love ("He who . . . does not receive my words, already has a judge, namely, the Word I have spoken to him", Jn. 12, 48).

It has to be said that, from the beginnings of Christianity till today no solemn teaching of the magisterium has so clearly brought out the importance of the essential eschatological aspects of the life of charity in the Church and its members, according to the New Testament, as the documents of the recent Council.[11] This is particularly true for the contemporary duties of that charity, as envisaged in the concrete by the Council.[12] No doubt, the messianic witness which this Christian charity must bear to the poor, this witness of their deliverance through Jesus, Messiah and Son of God, is far from being achieved. It must develop and expand from day to day. Elsewhere I have pointed out that, without underrating the gravity and urgency of the economic misery that Christians have a duty to relieve today, we should no less be concerned about the other, perhaps less spectacular, kinds of poverty of a human race that does

[11] Among other conciliar texts, see On the Church, 7 and 8, par. 5; On the Missions, 9; On Ecumenism, passim, and particularly, because of its nature and development, On the Church in the Modern World, 21, par. 3; 38; 39; 93.
[12] See On the Church, 2 (end); 5 (end); 6; 8 (end); 9, par. 2; ch. VII; 68; On the Missions, 9 and On Ecum., 24, etc.

not live by bread alone.[13] At the same time the Council has insisted more than the magisterium has ever done in the past that Christians should practice this precept of the Lord in the light of the new future toward which we are groping at present, and this means, where our faith is concerned, that we must act in the light of the Christian eschatological perspective.

The *Pastoral Constitution on the Church in the Modern World,* for instance, states that it is "obvious" that brotherly love is "of paramount importance to men growing daily more dependent on one another and to a world which is becoming more unified every day" (n. 24, par. 2). In fact, to give only one example, who does not see already that, without the brotherly love revealed to Christians by Jesus as the great motive force of the world's redemption, the irreversible process of universal socialization would lead the masses to the tyranny of a most inhuman technocracy? One could easily multiply such examples. If Christians can and indeed should be glad today, as in the early days of the Church, for that messianic deliverance which they experience in themselves and to which they bear witness by the practice of that divine *agape,* the present concrete historical situation makes them also realize the burden of their increased responsibility in the present frightening eschatological perspective. This tension is more than ever necessary to the sign of God's coming, which is their love for neighbor, a sign of messianic deliverance or of eschatological judgment.

III

What Shape Should Brotherly Love Take Today?

The question is: What is partly new in this Christian brotherly love so that it may be the sign of God's coming today in the world of today? I am not speaking here of those features that have been present in charity at all times, but rather of those psychological and moral elements that the present situation of

---

[13] "Pour une Eglise des Béatitudes de la pauvreté," *op. cit.,* pp. 190f.

the Church and the world seems to require in the practice of this brotherly love.

1. *From an Inter-Christian Love to a Universal Brotherhood*

If the analysis of the present situation in Church and world corresponds to the facts, the two first requirements of brotherly love today are bound to be a universally open missionary attitude and elasticity in its adaptation to the wide diversity of spiritual groupings with which it will seek communion and explore a dialogue of friendship.

In contrast with those times when brotherly love was usually practiced only among Christians (families, parishes, charitable works, etc.) while the "missionaries" in the old sense undertook practically alone to spread the Good News of God's presence in Jesus beyond the visible boundaries of the Church, today all Christians will have this mission to reveal the Gospel to these spiritual groupings, without having to go outside the framework of their daily lives. Thus, in every corner of the globe, they have to practice from day to day that brotherly love which manifests the presence of God. There will no longer be one Christian world contained within the boundaries of a geographical Christendom, and another world, unaware of God's presence in Jesus, beyond it. The "missionaries" will no longer have the monopoly of that many-sided evangelization which Christ entrusted to his Church. The present unification of the world will break down the last barriers between man and man, and Christian charity must bear witness to the presence of the God of light and love in their daily encounter with all kinds of spiritual groupings, whether of those who already share for a large part their faith, such as non-Catholic Christians, or of those who, while knowing of Jesus, refuse to accept that he is the Messiah or, *a fortiori,* the Son of the living God, such as the Jewish or Moslem communities, or those vast religious groups of deists or animists, who do not accept that God has revealed himself in history and still seek him only aided by man's

religious sense, or those other increasingly numerous groups
that reject the very notion of God, like the militant or non-
militant atheists.

It is at the heart of that mankind that Christians must live
more and more every day in faithfulness to that command of
brotherly love, given them by the master. History and the teaching of the Council converge on this point. It is therefore interesting that the *Constitution on the Church* has devoted important sections to each of these groupings in Chapter II, on
the People of God, and not, as no doubt most theologians would
have thought before the Council, in a separate chapter which
would not have integrated them in the mystery of the one People
of God. This was not accidental. It was the result of a clear
decision which, in itself as well as in the consequences for Christian charity, has been restated in several other documents, like
the Decrees on the *Lay Apostolate,* the *Missionary Activity of
the Church,* the *Eastern Churches* and *Ecumenism,* the Declarations on *Religious Freedom* and on *Non-Christian Religions,* and
particularly in the passages devoted to atheism in the *Pastoral
Constitution on the Church in the Modern World.*

In general, the Church of the Council has adopted the program of Charles de Foucauld: to be "the universal brother" has,
of all necessity, become the program of Christian love, over-
riding all particularism and protectionism which in fact pre-
vailed in the past.[14] This new situation, with its new missionary
responsibilities urgently demanding a reconsideration of the
Church's ministry in order to cope with it, has also been emphasized by the Council, particularly in its *Decree on the Pastoral
Office of Bishops in the Church*[15] and in its *Decree on the
Ministry and Life of Priests.*[16] At the end of this article I shall

[14] In his encyclical *Populorum Progressio* (n. 66f.) Paul VI speaks of
the need today for a "universal charity".

[15] *On the Bishops,* 13, par. 2, quoted below in the text. The attitude
described here is obviously not limited to the bishops. See *On the Missions,* 12, on the presence of Christian brotherly love in every human
society.

[16] *On the Ministry,* 6: "Christians should also be taught that they do
not live for themselves alone, but, according to the demands of the new

point out that this will probably soon bring about a new kind of relationship within the Church between committed Christians and those charged with apostolic functions.

2. Dialogue and Communion

These new conditions affecting the practice of brotherly love will develop a new exploration of the dialogue. Thus, for instance, the *Decree on the Pastoral Office of Bishops in the Church* says: "Since it is the mission of the Church to converse with the human society in which she lives, bishops especially are called upon to approach men, seeking and fostering dialogue with them. These conversations on salvation ought to be distinguished for clarity of speech as well as for humility and gentleness so that truth may always be joined with charity, and understanding with love. Likewise they should be characterized by due prudence allied, however, with that trustfulness which fosters friendship and thus is naturally disposed to bring about a union of minds." [17] This dialogue must take place wherever socialization affects human society,[18] with great personal respect,[19] particularly where religious truth is concerned.[20] It must be practiced within the Church,[21] particularly among priests,[22] but also outside with non-Catholic Christians,[23] with the Jews,[24] with non-Christian religions,[25] with atheists,[26] with the adver-

---

law of charity, every man must administer to others the grace he has received. In this way all will discharge in a Christian manner their duties within the community of men." And a little further on: "The local community should not only promote the care of its own faithful, but filled with a missionary zeal, it should also prepare the way to Christ for all men" (cf. *On the Missions,* 12 and *passim*).

[17] *On the Bishops,* 13, par. 2.
[18] *The Church in the Modern World,* 25.
[19] *Ibid.,* 18.
[20] *On Relig. Freedom,* 3, par. 2.
[21] *The Church in the World,* 56, par. 2; *On the Lay Apost.,* 25, par. 2.
[22] *On the Bishops,* 28; *On the Ministry,* 8.
[23] *On the Church,* 15; *On Ecum.,* 4, par. 2; 11, par. 1; 18; 22, par. 3.
[24] *On the Church,* 16; *On Non-Christian Rel.,* 2, 3.
[25] *On the Church,* 16; *On Non-Christian Rel.,* 1, 1; 2, 3; 4, 5; 5, 1-2.
[26] *On the Church,* 16; *On the Ch. in the Modern World,* 21, 6.

saries of the faith,[27] and in short, with all men[28] and among all nations.[29] This training for dialogue must therefore be given a prominent place in the formation of the laity,[30] the clergy,[31] and in the education given at Catholic universities.[32]

Through this dialogue and beyond it, all must seek the communion of friendship with others. It is an essential duty of bishops[33] and priests[34] to create this communion and friendship in the communities entrusted to their care. Religious superiors in the exercise of their function[35] and religious communities in their daily life[36] must apply themselves to this. Future priests must be trained for this[37] and the young must be brought up with this in their schools.[38] This pursuit of the communion of friendship is of course an essential part of family life.[39] It lies at the heart of all ecumenism.[40] According to the Council it should inspire relations with non-Christian religions.[41] The very prologue of the *Pastoral Constitution on the Church in the Modern World* demands that this be pursued with all men, and it remains the prevailing theme throughout this whole document.

3. *Building Up the Messianic People of God*

Integrated in the whole network of human relationships, charity is something that builds up (1 Cor. 8, 1; Rom. 15, 2). But it builds up with a purpose. For the believer the aim of the

[27] *On the Ch. in the Modern World*, 28, 1; 92, 5.
[28] *Ibid.*, 22, 5; 24, 1; 43, 5; 92 (whole); *On the Missions*, 12, 1; 38, 7; 41, 5; *On Chr. Educ.*, 8, 2.
[29] *On the Ch. in the Modern World*, 56, 2; 85, 3; 92, 1.
[30] *On the Lay Apost.*, 29, 5; 31.
[31] *On Priestly Training*, 19, 2.
[32] *On Chr. Educ.*, 1, 2; 11, 1; 12.
[33] *On the Bishops*, 13, 2; 16, 1; 28, 2; 36, 1.
[34] *Ibid.*, 30, 2 and 3; *On the Ministry*, 9.
[35] *On the Relig. Life*, 14, 3.
[36] *Ibid.*, 15, 1.
[37] *On Priestly Training*, 8; 9; 10, 1; 19, 2.
[38] *On Chr. Educ.*, 8, 3.
[39] *On the Ch. in the World*, 12, 4.
[40] *On Ecum., passim.*
[41] *On Non-Christian Rel.*, 1, 1; 2, 3; 4, 5; 6, 1 and 2, etc,

dialogue and the values of communion are all related to the mystery of God made man, which lies at the heart of their belief. It is this relationship with the mystery of Jesus which endows all reality with the quality of the Christian vision of the universe and of a Christian existence. Christian brotherly love does not pursue dialogue and communion as a kind of religious escape from the properly human vocation but rather in order to bring this vocation, embracing the whole human condition, to perfect fulfillment with the infinite dimensions of a divine vocation. For the believer, then, there are no limits to this dialogue and communion apart from falsehood, rejection and injustice. "According to the almost unanimous opinion of believers and unbelievers alike, all things on earth should be related to man as their center and crown." [42] In this human messianism through which man, in Jesus, accepts all things human within a divine perspective that keeps on breaking through all human limitations, the Council asserted: "Thus we are witnesses of the birth of a new humanism, one in which man is defined first of all by his responsibility toward his brothers and toward history." [43]

According to this teaching we must therefore specify that messianic man is so to speak the system of reference by which the believer perceives how to pursue this dialogue and communion with all. According to the Jesus revealed to us in Scripture, messianic man is therefore, all at once, the man who seeks and possesses prophetically all truth; who unfolds his kingly power with an efficacy that aims at nothing less than the fulfillment of creation itself; who, as priest, strives after all justice, all redemption and all sanctity. As prophet, king and priest Jesus is the head of that Church, which, already sharing through faith in his messianic plenitude, has as its mission to "recapitulate" (Eph. 1, 10) eschatologically all things in this messianic and divine mystery of Jesus. And it does so precisely by that effective brotherly love which seeks to bring about that com-

[42] *On the Ch. in the World*, 12, 1.
[43] *Ibid.*, 55 (end).

munion of all along the lines of prophecy, kingship and priesthood which constitute its messianism.

IV

BROTHERLY LOVE IN THE CHURCH

All that has been said no doubt applies to all Christians, but
in the first place to the laity who, "by their very vocation, seek
the kingdom of God by engaging in temporal affairs and by
ordering them according to the plan of God. They live in the
world, that is, in each and in all of the secular professions and
occupations. They live in the ordinary circumstances of family
and social life, from which the very web of their existence is
woven. They are called there by God so that by exercising their
proper function and being led by the spirit of the Gospel they
can work for the sanctification of the world from within, in the
manner of leaven." [44] Something has therefore to be said about
the demands which the Christian laity will inevitably make
within the Church, particularly with regard to their relations
with those in charge of the apostolic ministry, if their charity and
witness are to be that leaven in the world.

1. *"Clergy and Laity" or "the Disciples and the Twelve"*

The tension between the universal expansion of brotherly
love and the institutional position of those who must ensure
this expansion in today's world shows certain new aspects which
the Church's authorities should take very seriously. No doubt,
the distinction between those who are and those who are not
"ordained" to the apostolic ministry is and always will be essential to the institutional structure of the Church. Chapters II and
III of the *Constitution on the Church* are both necessary. Of
these two, Chapter IV is however the newer in outlook, and
some changes will be necessary in the relations between the
members of the Church and the ministers, relations which have
varied considerably in the past.

[44] *On the Church*, 31.

In the documents of the early Church and before Constantine we find that, before the pair "clergy-laity" became common, there were other pairs in use in the opposite order: "disciples-the Twelve", or "disciples-ministers", or "disciples-pastors", and so on. The Church appeared first of all as the community of believers. If the Twelve and their successors already exercised by apostolic institution the three indispensable ministries of Word, pastoral care and cult, it was essentially as a service to that community of believers. The active part this community played in the very appointment of the ministers was one way among others of signifying this type of relationship. Here, as on so many other points, the Council deliberately left the past behind and in the texts dealing with the responsibility of the laity as with those concerning the irreplaceable functions of bishops, priests and deacons, urges us to envisage the relations between clergy and laity in a way which comes closer to those that existed at the beginning. The laity are emphatically encouraged to exercise their own functions in the world and in the Church to the full. The clergy are asked to concentrate more exclusively and more competently on their triple ministry of the Word, which nourishes prophecy in the Church, of pastoral care which presides over charity in the community, and of liturgical worship which integrates, from baptism to the eucharist, the whole life of Christians in the world into the Passover of Jesus. One should not look so much at details in the text but try to see beyond them that there is here a beginning of a change in the relationship between clergy and laity in the sense of a closer adaptation to the Gospel.

If this is true, one may foresee for today's Church a period of increasing "declericalization" accompanied by a new style of life less sociologically differentiated from that of the ordinary faithful, but also marked by a more exclusive concentration on specifically apostolic labor in the service of the community. In order that the brotherly love of the laity can be, in society, that leaven of all human striving after truth, relevancy, justice and peace, the brotherly love of the clergy must be more exclusively devoted to the life of the Christian community. In this way the laity will learn to see their problems in the light of the faith, to maintain among themselves an unfailing charity in the midst of the tensions of this world, and to consecrate their many-sided activity in the world to the only perfect worship of Christ on the cross. Unless the inner life of the Church is renewed in this way, the increasing secularization of life in the world will endanger the faith (prophecy), charity (kingship) and sanctity (priesthood) of the Christian laity: "Most men's love will grow cold" (Mt. 24, 12).

2. *A Church of Dialogue and Communion*

All this means that within the Church itself the new aspects of brotherly love, required by the present situation, must become manifest. If every Christian or Christian group must be a sign of the presence of God's love among men through the pursuit of dialogue and communion of friendship, how much more must the collective Church appear, first of all, not as a powerful international organization, still less a more or less inhuman anonymous society, concerned only with itself, but as a truly fraternal community, "poor and serving",[45] a "communion".[46] By constantly speaking of "services" rather than "powers" in connection with the functions of episcopacy,[47] priesthood [48] and diaconate,[49] the Council has laid down firmly the principles of such a transformation of all those elements in the institutional life of the Church which are, even today, still derived from the Christian past rather than from the apostolic institution as given by Jesus and the Twelve. It is urgently necessary to draw the consequences from these principles, not only to ensure faithfulness to the Word of God, but also to cope with the demands of Christian brotherly love in today's world, that is, if one really

[45] Y. M. J. Congar, *Pour une Eglise servante et pauvre* (Paris, 1963).
[46] J. Hamer, *L'Eglise est une communion* (Paris, Unam Sanctam, 1963).
[47] *On the Church*, III, *passim; On the Bishops,* 16.
[48] *On the Church*, 28; *On the Ministry, passim.*
[49] *On the Church,* 29.

wants Christians, individually and collectively, to be an effective witness to the presence of God.

3. Christian Communities on a Human Scale

It seems to me that the most important and most urgent of the institutional changes at present is to have Christian communities at ground level which are genuinely human in practice. As Christians today must be fully committed in their brotherly love to life in a world that is becoming less and less Christian, they need the support of an ecclesial life adjusted to the scale of human existence. Neither the anemic parish of a de-Christianized countryside, nor the overblown parish of urban agglomerations can any longer provide a genuine community life for their members. Such parishes cannot function as prophetic communities where they can learn to apply the light of the faith to the increasingly difficult problems thrown up by the numerous attitudes and philosophies of a non-Christian and even atheistic world. Such parishes are not genuinely royal communities of unfailing charity and friendship where their brotherly love can find the missionary strength required for their witness in this world. Nor are they communities of redemption and sanctification where Christians can fully exercise their function of priestly mediation. In the various movements of Catholic Action as in the missionary movements of the last decades experience has shown that the more Christians are driven by their love to insert their witness at the very heart of the world and its development, the more they feel the need of being rooted in a true Christian community where they can commune with one another in the specific values which such a community provides. This experience may well extend gradually to Christians in general as they become more conscious of their minority situation and that missionarry vocation which the Council has outlined for the laity. This will demand an urgent re-assessment of the Church's institutions at ground level. I have already pointed this out elsewhere in connection with Christian inter-aid and the relief of every kind of poverty within and outside the

Church. What I have said there applies to all three essential aspects of the Christian community which I have elaborated here.[50]

CONCLUSION

We are now in a transition period from a brotherly love lived mainly within the Christian communities constituting a "Christendom" to a brotherly love firmly interwoven with the life of every human collective existence, including the temporal aspect, with respect for their legitimate autonomy. We are passing from a Church which was a "Christendom", an institutional structure of society, even at the temporal level, to a Church which is forced by the present historical situation to become more and more purely itself, that is, messianic and divine, in order to be, by the radiation of its charity, the effective witness to the presence of the God of love in today's world.

If, finally, we look at this historical situation and this development in the light of revelation, we see that, far from being the product of the "evil of our days", they lead to a greater respect for the distinction between the order of Caesar and that of God as taught by Jesus, and, by the same token, to a more valid manifestation of the transcendence and immanence of the God of love.

Nor does this development endanger the universality of God's salvific will (1 Tim. 2, 4) in Christ the Savior and in the Church in which he unfolds the fullness of his divine and human mystery (Eph. 1, 23). Who would have thought after the frequent commentaries of not so long ago on the words: "No salvation outside the Church" (strictly true in itself), that the Council would underline the efficacy of the "sacrament of salvation", which is the Church,[51] far beyond its visible boundaries as the evangelical leaven in the world (Mt. 13, 33; Lk. 13, 20-21)?

In the present growth of the demands of brotherly love as in

---

[50] "Pour une Eglise des Béatitudes de la pauvreté," *op. cit.,* pp. 263f.
[51] *On the Church,* 48, 2.

the present historical demand made on the Church to center everything, even its institutional life, on the service of this love, our faith, nourished on the Word of God, sees here at work the mystery of that "remnant" which, in the midst of that general apostasy at the end of time (Mt. 24, 9-13 and 15-25; Lk. 18, 8; 2 Thess. 2, 3-4 and 9-12; Apoc. 13; Jn. 16, 2-4), will achieve through love the victory of the cross of Jesus, the wisdom and power of God (1 Cor. 1, 24).

Hans Urs von Balthasar/*Basle, Switzerland*

Immediate Relationship with God

Few phrases are as suspect to anyone who thinks honestly and soberly as: "This or that is nothing but . . ." Life and spirit are nothing but a complicated structure of matter. The moral good is nothing but what is useful or agreeable to the individual or society. Aestheticism is nothing but a branch of sociology. So-called evil is nothing but the expression of a biological condition. Such glib formulas, often presented as "debunking" definitions, are still current in vast numbers. To this category belongs unfortunately also a slogan which, consciously or subconsciously, explicitly or implicitly, is very popular among Christians and theologians, and which, briefly, runs: True religion is nothing but ethics. This means that the right relation to God is nothing but the right relation to neighbor (including oneself).

It is admitted that such a simplification demands some manipulating of history since this phrase has never been valid in the ages which preceded our own. If it is accepted today it is either because religion (as closeness to God) was formerly a valid notion but has lost this validity today through the transformation of the world and the disappearance of God from a humanity which thinks in terms of technology and sociology, or because it was already in the past a fatal error, an intellectual illusion from which this modern age has delivered us. God has become an unknown being (and in this sense, is "dead"). God never existed (and is therefore "dead"). Religion has become ethics and can only have meaning as ethics. This seems to provide solid common ground for the "dialogue with atheism". And this holds particularly for Christians who are told that the "new(!) commandment is to show their specific 'faith' by an intensive practice of the love of neighbor which will distinguish them".

We have reason to mistrust this new application of the "glib formula". That there is a partial truth in most of these formulas one does not deny. In this case it is true that all religion is certainly also ethics, and Christian religion is this preeminently. Aquinas explains it as follows: "Religion has two kinds of activity. The first comprises actions that are properly and directly religious and are performed as such; through these actions man is related exclusively to God, as in sacrifice or adoration. The other kind of actions are performed through virtues controlled by religion insofar as these are performed in view of our awe of God; these are religious acts because the virtue concerned with the ultimate end dominates and influences all other virtues which relate things to this ultimate end. In this sense the visiting of orphans and widows in their affliction (Jas. 1, 27) is an act of religion, although the act proceeds immediately from the virtue of mercy. And to keep oneself unstained from the world (*ibid.*) is also an act of religion, although it proceeds immediately from self-discipline or some such virtue" (IIa IIae, q. 81, a 1 ad 1). Before dealing with the issues raised by this summary statement, let us look at another point.

Guardini likes to distinguish three zones in human reality: the zone of human nature, which he knows and recognizes without difficulty also in the state of "fallenness", of disintegration and alienation; the zone of grace with its hidden truths and laws, which is only accessible to the man who is willing to receive it in faith; then a third zone of relations with the created world which only become clear in the light of supernatural grace, first of all and naturally, to the faithful who let themselves be guided by this light, and then to wider groupings of humanity when, through the believer, they have been proposed, tested and made credible after they have penetrated man's consciousness. A clear example of this is the history of the *Declaration of Human Rights* (if we limit ourselves to recent history). In it and in Jefferson's *Declaration of Independence* (1776) we find, on the basis of a Christian interpretation of human dignity, that "all men are by nature equally free and independent, and have certain inherent rights". This the French developed on the lines of Enlightenment in 1789. The German Constitution, after mentioning God, begins by laying down that human dignity is inviolable and "the foundation of every human community" and then derives the basic human rights from this principle.[1] The dignity of the individual person as the image of God is seen in the light of revelation and is thus shown as evident to all mankind, a precarious possession which can at any time be obscured again wherever the light of Christianity threatens to disappear. But wherever this light prevails directly or indirectly, the foundation of ethics is seen not to be exclusively the common good but primarily the good of the person, and ethics becomes consequently the fulfillment of an existential dialogue, between person and person, in recognition of the absolute value of "thou" over against "I". This principle of dialogue does not rest as such on revelation. It regulates for an important part the natural ethics of human intercourse, but is deepened and strengthened by a religion which sees the God-man relationship also as a dialogue between persons.

In the light of these distinctions the question arises for a Christian whether, from the Christian point of view, an immediate relationship between God and the individual is possible and necessary for our time, both factually and historically, or whether it is perhaps an obstacle to, and a misrepresentation of, the essence of Christianity when we make this immediate relationship with God the primary, or even exclusive, element in

[1] W. Wertenbruch, "Menschenrechte," in *Rel. in Gesch. u. Gegenw.*, 3rd ed., Vol. IV (1960), pp. 870f.

human intercourse. We shall discuss this on three levels: (1) the central relationship between Jesus Christ and God; (2) the distance between Christ, the God-man, and us human beings; and (3) the possible and real compatibility of this distance with an inward participation in our relationship with God.

1. *The Relationship between Jesus and God*

It is quite possible to see in Jesus' relationship with God the supreme fulfillment of what, in olden times, was felt as man's immediate religious relationship with God. This possibility is seen more clearly when we trace the stages of relationship with God in the Old Testament from the beginning of mankind to Christ.

That man recognizes by nature an ethical sphere which does not coincide with the religious sphere lies in his elementary and ineluctable knowledge of the fact that he owes his existence not to himself, nor completely to his parents, since they and all previous generations are basically in the same situation as himself: they are not the cause of their own existence. The emergence of the individual being from the generative forces of the world is surrounded by mystery, the mystery of the immense power of these forces to pass on life with all its darkness and brightness, to set it free in one way or other, to accompany it from far or near and finally to let it sink back into themselves at death. The beginning and end of what is ephemeral, dependent, not-absolute, lie in a region beyond our imagination. We can give it a name and an image, yet we cannot understand it although we owe our existence to it and surrender ourselves to it. Both these acts, this owing and this surrender, are somehow existentially presupposed, even if we refuse rebelliously to cooperate with them consciously. These two acts do not depend either on whether we credit this mystery of the ground of our being with personality or not. The very changeability of mythical explanations, of divinities and divine names, may show that even in olden times man did not cling, deep inside himself, to a single explanation but experienced the myths as the changing appearance of the one mystery.

The ethics of such religious cultures, whether primitive or advanced, were wholly permeated by religion in that people enacted the drama of their collective life before the same divine mystery (even if only related to their own society), and expressed the sense of their dependence on the divine even in the particular activities of their communal life, their politics, economics, law and medicine. When we pass from this stage to the modern world one can of course say that this childlike and inarticulate dependence on the divinity expressed their inability to organize themselves, free and technically equipped for the control of nature. Yet, the progress toward human adulthood in the shaping of man's life and man's world has changed nothing in this decisive human structure contained in that basic "owing" and "surrender" of man. Within the sphere of this world, adulthood does not solve the question how anything that exists rises from this incomprehensible ground of being and always sinks back into it. The religious question is existentially as deeply embodied in what is finite as before, in spite of the fact that we consciously push it into the background and ignore it in the light of the imposing task of collective control of the world.

In the Old Testament the experience and self-awareness of Israel show this incomprehensible ground of being as a living, choosing, saving and covenanting God. There is a change in his incomprehensibility: he has become something positive, near, and demanding with "jealousy" for the sake of grace. Since he has chosen and redeemed a people that is distinguished by nothing, in a way which is beyond understanding and reason, he claims a disinterested and exclusive response. This passionately exclusive mutual relationship between God and people is called love by Hosea and soon after in Deuteronomy. It is a love of married partners or a love between father and son. This relationship seemed hard to Israel, and there was frequent and increasingly radical denial of it, but it also seemed infinitely wonderful and a source of happiness so that they sang it throughout the centuries in songs of gratitude and praise in a way which no other people could even approach, and these songs bear witness to a most immediate relationship with God. This praise is praise of God for his own sake and not primarily to obtain something. It is a praise which is based on the baselessness of divine grace in its elective love. Only inasmuch as the people as a whole are the possession of God, did God put his seal on this people's life and law. Human law has to adjust itself to God's notion of what is right (*sedaqa, mišpat*). It is not merely a matter of God issuing "positively" a moral and juridical code of covenant, but with it goes a concept of negotiation which is rooted in the very event of the covenant: "It was not because you were more in number than any other people that the Lord set his love upon you and chose you, for you were the fewest of all peoples, but it is because the Lord loves you." "Beware lest you say in your heart, 'My power and the might of my hand have gotten me this wealth.' " "Do not say in your heart, 'It is because of my righteousness that the Lord has brought me in to possess this land.' " "For the Lord your God is God of gods and Lord of lords, the great, the mighty, and the terrible God, who is not partial and takes no bribe. He executes justice for the fatherless and the widow and loves the sojourner, giving him food and clothing. Love the sojourner therefore for you were sojourners in the land of Egypt." "If there is among you a poor man, you shall not harden your heart, but you shall open your hand to him, and lend him sufficient for his need, whatever it may be." "You shall remember that you were a slave in the land of Egypt, and the Lord your God redeemed you." "You shall not abhor an Edomite, for he is your brother; you shall not abhor an Egyptian, because you were a sojourner in his land." "You shall not take a widow's garment in pledge; but you shall remember that you were a slave in Egypt and that the Lord your God redeemed you from there." [2]

This whole system of social ethics is very clearly summarized

[2] Dt. 7, 7f.; 7, 17; 9, 4; 10, 17-9; 15, 7f. and 15; 23, 7; 24, 17f.

in Jesus' parable of the ungrateful servant: he who has received much, must himself give what little he is in remembrance of grace received. This is what is called God's law in Israel. The shocking social conditions, castigated by Amos and Isaiah, cry to heaven precisely because they are directly sins against the covenanted love.

Jesus understood and presented himself as the fulfillment of the old covenant,[3] and even as its embodiment. Just as he is the absolute choice of God, the absolute promise of his love and his unfailing loyalty (2 Cor. 1, 19ff.), so he is what seemed impossible to the old covenant, the recapitulation of all the standard figures among the people: founder, lawgiver, judge, king, prophet, servant of Yahweh, the heavenly son of man, the scapegoat, the high priest . . . In every one of these positions he gave to God *existentially* that perfect praise that the psalmists gave mainly only in words. But his position is also there where God, from his glory, sends the fire of his wrath down on Jerusalem (Ez. 10, 6); he also embodies all that must be destroyed and damned, and thus carries the covenant through the fire of judgment. This incomprehensible combination lifts him above the ranks of all human beings, however blessed. He is not merely an example, but the original image (*Urbild*). His existence embraces all human reactions within the covenant and is at the same time the whole deed-and-Word of God embodied in man.

This explains the characteristics which doubtless and beyond all theological explanation are his: (1) an unprecedented child-like intimacy with God as his Father (Abba) from whom his whole existence derives its life, and in whose power and by whose commission he does all that he has to do; (2) a constant return to the solitude, silence and depth of prayer where he draws not only the power of his Word and wondrous deeds but

[3] This is repeated with various nuances in all evangelists and Paul. The sharp conflict with the pharisees and scribes frees the hagiographer from any suspicion of having re-interpreted the image of Jesus to make it fit in with the old covenant. He has quietly put himself in a position where all images converge upon him quite naturally.

also the concentrated fullness which flows from there into the gospels, from the existential Word into the theological Word.

This immediate relationship of Jesus to the Father (in the light of union or in the darkness of the cross) enables him to show his existence to the world as the total incarnation of God's love. It enables him, in Karl Barth's words, to let himself become "man *for* all men", as opposed to us who as creatures can only be men *with* other men. If he had not penetrated so far into solitude with God he would never have gone so far ahead in communion with man. As he identifies himself, through this intimacy with the Father, with the Father's sheer love, he can turn the whole of his existence into "eucharistia", a eucharist in which his absolute "owing" of his origin and existence to God coincides with his absolute self-surrender to God in death. It is this comprehensive act, primarily addressed to the Father, which becomes the highest gift of love to man, namely, the gift of the Father's love. Jesus sees himself in his love as the tangible mediator of this gift of the Father. As he lets the Father turn him into a gift to man through an obedience which is identical with his love, he reaches man in his most inward reality and obtains man from his Father as his brother. "Here am I, and the children God has given me" (Heb. 2, 13).

I cannot expatiate here on the endless ramifications of this mystery which is opened up here and from which the whole of dogma is unfolded. I can only indicate what is necessary for the present purpose: in Jesus all that was immediate relationship with God in natural religion or in man's existence under the old covenant is fulfilled in a supreme and incomparable manner.

I have already briefly mentioned in connection with "religion" that the immediate relationship with God in religious activity is obscured by the modern understanding of the world but cannot be explained away. For man will always "owe" his existence to this ultimate mystery and "surrender" himself to it. Still less can the modern attitude diminish the Christian relationship with God insofar as it is based on Jesus' relationship with the Father. The two following points will make this still clearer.

2. *The Distance between Jesus and Us*

In order to be totally man *for* men, Jesus is not primarily man *with* men. He is this certainly and even fundamentally, insofar as his mission demands this: "He eats with tax collectors and sinners" (Mt. 9, 11). But his mission to do these things stems from the Father. He is himself this mission, this "Word" of the Father addressed to the sinners. In order to be this he had to "empty" himself and "humble" himself in absolute obedience (Phil. 2, 7f.), so that the awe-inspiring majesty of the "I" of the covenant became transparent in him. "You have heard that it was said to the men of old . . . But I say to you . . ." (Mt. 5, 21f.). One should not see a "dialogue situation" in the conclusion of the covenant on Mount Sinai where God appeared in the visible attributes of his glory and "the people were afraid and trembled and stood afar off" (Ex. 20, 18; Dt. 5, 23f.). God takes the stage, *he* acts in word and deed, and man is required to respond in utter obedience.

Something of this glory of Sinai hovers around the humble Son of Man when, in the name of his Father, he brings the two-edged sword of God's love into the world: "From his mouth issued a sharp two-edged sword" (Apoc. 1, 16), the sword of judgment and redemption. The origin of the communication established by him lies in complete solitude. It is the *leit motif* of his life. It touched him at twelve years of age when he did not trouble, out of obedience to *his* Father, to inform his family—this is not exactly the procedure of a dialogue. Later he made no allowance for his mother and relatives when they came to visit him. And finally, when abandoned on the cross by his Father, he plainly also abandoned his mother, referring her to another son, so that she, too, should play her bitter part in the sphere in which he himself had lived and acted.

Christ always and obviously presupposes the sphere of human society with its natural dialogue situation as a creaturely condition. It functions somehow within itself: married life with its erotic "one-flesh situation", founded by God (Mt. 19, 6); family life which, with its own set of laws, enforces a certain form of goodness ("If you then, who are evil, know how to give good gifts to your children . . ." Mt. 7, 11); pleasant conduct toward friends ("Do not Gentiles do the same?"); the return of love to those that love us ("Do not tax collectors do the same?" Mt. 5, 46f.), and so on. All this is recognized as the sphere of "eros" in the broader sense, on which "agape", the love of God, descends out of the "solitude" and where it proclaims its ineffable mystery in the utter solitude of the cross, the mystery of the absolute dialogue which takes place within the Trinity. It is this dialogue which, through the mission of Jesus, must become the inner form of the human dialogue (Eph. 5, 21-33; Phil. 2, 5f.; Col. 3, 12-17, etc.). But this can only happen through a sharing in the solitude of the incarnate Word. In order to give *all* love, one must renounce all love on the cross, not only the love of loveless sinners but also that of the loving Church (in Mary) and of the Father himself. Without this abandoning of all, the Christian gift of all is impossible.

Given that Christ's true mission was to bring the love of the Father into the hour of darkness, into the utter non-love of the world, there arises a situation ostensibly similar and analogous to the emotions of dialogue, but which at heart is quite different. We can call this the confrontation situation, the confrontation of opposed protagonists, the clash of one head against another.[4] Jesus' attitude in these circumstances is determined not by the impression he makes on the human "thou", as if to say that this "thou" (in Kant's sense of "noumenal", as personal representative of the categorical imperative) could summon him to reflection, conversion and generosity. Rather is his attitude determined by the inexorable nature of the Father's love, in pursuit of which, and on the sinner's behalf, there is nothing at which he will stop. His human situation is no less existential than that of Buber, Ebner, Jaspers, and others; it is merely different. It is precisely this being exposed of the whole heart to the "thou" of human fellowship, but tending toward martyrdom. This was best understood by Kierkegaard (in the diary of

[4] Not: "tête-à-tête" but "tête contre tête".

his last years). Because Jesus is prepared to die out of love for the Father's love, he can show in his polemical discourses this hardness of merciless exposure and accusations. The very Spirit of eternal love assumes for this the part of the prosecutor in court (Jn. 16, 8-11). And yet, this *agape* must become the inward form of all inter-human relationships, whether erotic or otherwise. Christianity is truly the religion of absolute love. But while we can guess the function of Jesus in the establishment of this new love, the imitation required of the Christian as an integration of *agape* into *eros* seems incomprehensible to us.

3. *Participation in the Specific Love of Christ at a Distance*

When the whole distance of the analogy of being between God's love and human love seems to have been overcome by the existence of Christ, this is no excuse for the Christian to abandon all effort. "Let him remain what he is, the God-man, the man for other men, but let him allow us to be what we are, simple men together with other men. Let him reconcile us to the Father with his immediate relationship, but let him allow us to find God where it fits in with the situation of created persons: in the dialogue with our fellowmen." To speak like this means that the threshold which leads to the reality of Christianity has not yet been crossed. In Christian terms we can only say: we can and must "reflect the glory of the Lord" (*katoptrizesthai;* 2 Cor. 3, 18 [5] in all social situations, since we have obtained the glory of his love and grace first of all in a situation of solitude, utterly without dialogue. We can develop this first in predominantly Protestant terms, and then expand it in the Catholic sense.

(a) The Protestant will here point, first of all, to a *factual* (not temporal) priority of the act of justification over that of sanctification (where Christian love then bestirs itself as love of neighbor.[6] It is, before all human activity, only the act of God

[5] For further explanation see J. Dupont, "Le chrétien miroir de la gloire divine d'après II Cor. 3, 18," in *Rev. Bibl.* 56 (1949), pp. 392-411.

[6] K. Barth, "Rechtfertigung und Heiligung," in *Zwischen den Zeiten* (1927), pp. 281-309.

which applies grace and appeals to the sinner through the cross of Christ. To this pure gift of God corresponds on the human side, according to Luther's theology, that pure faith which we can describe as the pure recognition of the absolute priority of the God of grace, as the mere reception in ourselves of God's justification, in which I can take no active part. Thus there were already in the Old Testament purely one-sided interventions of God, as in the promise to Abraham and later to David, and at the conclusion of the covenant on Mount Sinai. Nowhere was man consulted about this covenant, although the opposite is true for the *content* of this divine intervention: Abraham's faith implies the duty of obedience, tested on Moriah; the covenant of Sinai implies the obligation of sanctity, of observance of the "commandments, precepts and customs of God", and the promise to David also implies its conditions.

The defect in Luther's theology lies principally in that it separates too much a justifying faith from love (which is put with the "works") for polemical reasons.[7] For it is difficult to see why the originally pure faith, which already rests as such on pure grace, should not already be the first basic act of man's unconditional surrender to God.[8]

(b) This same situation can be expressed in a different way, which holds for both Catholic and Protestant, as the priority of the pure hearing of the Word before any personal human reaction to it. Since this "hearing" concerns the Word of God, it embraces the whole of man and the content of the Word surpasses essentially the created scope of the mind. It therefore presupposes man's total readiness to "listen", to "hear" with his whole soul and all his powers, to accept the content as God's truth, with an all-embracing openness, to exclude any "prejudice" (pre-judgment) and not to think to know anything already beforehand (for instance, what God should or should not say to "modern man"). "Hear, Israel, thus speaks the Lord thy God."

[7] Cf. P. Hacker, *Das Ich im Glauben bei Martin Luther* (Styria Graz, 1966), Ch. 4, "Liebe als Gesetzeswerk."

[8] This is not ruled out by the possibility of lasting faith being separated from lost love in the state of sin.

This basic biblical demand was interpreted in the Christian Middle Ages in the sense that all Christian action must flow from a preceding act of contemplation. Later Ignatius of Loyola interpreted it in a more biblical sense: at the origin of any specific Christian task lies an act of absolute indifference rooted in the immediate nearness of God, an act of total readiness for all things, whatever God may put into his Word. And this comes very close to Luther's pure faith. It always reflects what Jesus required of his disciples: to put themselves in principle beyond any inter-human relationship: "If anyone comes to me and does not hate his own father and mother and wife and children and brothers and sisters, yes, and even his own life, he cannot be my disciple" (Lk. 14, 26). "Hating" here means to abandon if necessary, to transcend in order to accept it all again from the Lord and so to transform all through the Word of God. This "listening", "contemplation" or "indifference" of pure acceptance is without any doubt the basis of all prayer, which is only truly prayer when it rests on the unconditional acceptance of God's will (or at least tries to rest on this acceptance). And one may say that wherever this acceptance is present in man or in a human situation, even when not admitted, or secret, but yet basically present, there is basically prayer.

(c) To put this into explicitly Catholic terms, one may say that participation in the mission and pattern of Christ's existence is possible, in spite of the remaining difference between him and us, whenever a believer is prepared to receive and to live his existence as a mission in the acceptance of his faith. This, according to Paul, is the structure of the Church's existence: not to arrange and pick out one's mission in some "adult" fashion but to accept the assignation of it from God in the "analogy of faith" (Rom. 12, 3) and "according to the measure of Christ's gift" (Eph. 4, 7 and 11f.). Then Luther's division of justification (faith) and sanctification (works) can correspond with the division of acceptance (of all things, Lk. 1, 38) and being sent (to some specific end) for the benefit of Church and mankind. Acceptance is the cross and dying with Christ; being sent in his power and spirit is to rise again with him (Rom. 6). But we must remember that a mission depends in *every* phase on the sender and can constantly be interfered with, while that act of immediate readiness for God (faith, hearing, silence and acceptance) must never become a thing of the past.

From the Christian point of view, a human "thou" can *remind* me often seriously and actively of God's demand and make it present to me, but as such (i.e. as a created "thou") it can never be the measure of God's demand on me in Christ. Men are most often considerate toward one another out of a sinful connivance, and the sinner himself is usually most considerate toward the sinner. In his demand for love God is indeed kind and forbearing, but not considerate, and the real mission of the Christian is measured by the measure of divine love. It is therefore in its origin and lasting structure immediately related to God and above dialogue. The first is produced by the Christian love of neighbor, which is, in the eyes of the world, always rare, vexatious and hardly explicable. Insofar as it is a participation in the love of God (the God-man) it breaks through the average love of "dialogue", and as such must implicitly work as hubris or pharisaism if not immediately combined with the humility of pure faith, which makes it credible for others: this is not what *I* can do, not *my* love, but the love of God in Christ, which I try to transmit (rather poorly than rightly), as my mission. This humility of faith must implicitly manifest the theological analogy of being, the distance between the justifying God and the unworthy, justified sinner. In Paul's mission and life we can study how the *agape* beyond dialogue of the apostolic mission goes to work in the dialogue of human *eros* (in natural human love). There is no way of discussing with these communities the Christian demands which it is his mission to present and work out. He demolishes every obstacle and demands pure obedience in the name of Christ (2 Cor. 10, 5f.). But he does so in a wonderful solidarity of love with his brethren. This makes him lay himself open to them instead of locking himself up in an inaccessible officialdom, and makes him ready to translate his mission that is beyond dialogue into a situation of genuine dialogue. This difficulty seems insolvable in terms of purely human psychology, and yet we see, as in 2 Corinthians, that it can be existentially lived with without any contortion.

Whoever wants to live the Christian life must first be with Christ in immediate relation to God and "die". Hence, all those who are sent by God always come from some desert. Christ came out of thirty years of obscurity and forty days of struggle in the desert where God is near. John the Baptist came from the desert. Paul spent three years in Arabia. God himself leads man "into the wilderness of the peoples" where he "will enter into judgment with him face to face . . . and make him pass under the rod . . . by number" (Ez. 20, 35-37). And many, tired and discouraged by the flood of prayerless talk in present Christianity, will, like Elijah, go into the desert, and there unexpectedly arrive on God's Horeb where he will encounter God in untrammelled nearness in order to be sent to the brethren with new tasks to fulfill.

Peter Steinfels/*New York, N.Y.*

Christian Conscience in America and the War in Vietnam

The American debate about Vietnam is confused and impassioned; nonetheless one can discern four main approaches to comprehending and criticizing U.S. policy.

1. *The* Pacifist *Approach*

For the absolute pacifist, the immorality of this war is an *a priori* conviction. His moral duty is to reveal this fact. His approach to the evidence is essentially illustrative. He must expose the suffering, the brutality and the duplicity the war involves. Since he is primarily concerned with the morality of the agent which represents him, he stresses the faults of his own government. But the faults of the enemy would not, in fact, disprove his case; at bottom, they reinforce it. War engenders cruelty. It cannot result in good.

2. *The* Legal *Approach*

The legalist looks to "formal criteria of a juridical nature by which the permissible behavior of States can be defined". Hence the involved arguments in the U.S. about the precise nature of the Geneva Agreements and America's assent to them. Opponents of the war point to the lack of U.N. sanction or argue that the action is unconstitutional since war has never been declared formally. The government talks of the SEATO[1] pact and various pledges made to South Vietnamese governments. Opposing committees of lawyers indict or absolve the U.S. on grounds of international laws. Behind the legal arguments is a strong moral impulse and a national tradition—the whole Wilsonian outlook on international affairs. Once the legal rights and wrongs are established, other considerations are secondary.

3. *The* Internationalist-Realist *Approach*

It accepts notions such as "national interest", "balance of power", and "spheres of influence" as being indispensable—and therefore moral—in a less-than-perfect world. Frankly accepting the role of power in international relations, it is a critique of both pacifism and legalism; as such it is suspected of providing a rationalization for cynical and ruthless "power politics". Yet, recognizing the necessity of compromise, it is also a critique of total war and the crusade mentality; as such it is welcomed as supporting moderation and negotiation.

If the internationalist-realist approach pays closest attention to the details of the evidence, it has severe limitations in mobilizing public opinion. In a contest between independent scholars and government experts, the general public tends to grant the latter the benefit of any doubt. Furthermore, the internationalist-realist approach shies away from unilateral actions, especially by major powers. Always postulating some sort of negotiating process, formal or informal, it has naturally led deep into debates over the failure of Washington and Hanoi to arrange negotiations.

4. *The* Revolutionist *Approach*

International politics are an extension of the dynamics of national revolutions. The morality of one's position is basically determined by alignment with either the revolutionary or counter-

---

[1] SEATO—*S*outh *E*ast *A*sian *T*reaty *O*rganization, founded in 1954 by the U.S., England, France, Australia, New Zealand, Thailand, Philippines and Pakistan to defend South-East Asia and the Pacific.

revolutionary forces. For opponents of the American intervention, the National Liberation Front is the force in Vietnam representing either the will of the people or the possibility of economic modernization; the U.S. has intervened because, out of capitalist self-preservation or psychological obsession with Communism, it is generally led to suppress revolutionary forces throughout the world. The supporters of the government's policy are apt to see revolution in terms of loss of freedom rather than nationalist manifestation or mobilization for development. They too see Vietnam as part of a wider policy of preventing Communists from amputating part of the "free world" or upsetting world order.

Religious response to the war has employed all of these approaches. Pacifist groups like the Protestant Fellowship of Reconciliation and the Catholic Peace Fellowship were prominent in the early anti-war protests. As well as the brutality of the war, they tended to stress the illegality of American intervention, the illegitimacy of various Saigon governments and the right of the Vietnamese to self-determination without outside interference. Advocates of the just-war theory or the internationalist-realist approach were originally concerned mainly with the means of warfare employed by the U.S. and South Vietnamese. They voiced concern over the use of torture, the large number of civilian deaths, and the possibility of indiscriminate air attacks. Many joined the agitation for negotiations; and, while not adopting the pacifist position, they frequently rallied to the defense of pacifist dissenters such as the young men who burned their draft cards or Father Daniel Berrigan, S.J., whose superiors sent him to Latin America to halt his anti-war activities.

The first phase of the Vietnam debate culminated in the Spring of 1965: in April, 2,500 clergymen signed an open letter to President Johnson demanding a cease-fire and negotiations, and in May the nationally televised teach-in took place in Washington. But meanwhile, two other events occurred which eventually sent the debate into a new phase, both more frustrating and more radical.

The first event was the President's declaration that the U.S. was willing to enter "unconditional" negotiations. From now on, critics asking anything less than unilateral withdrawal had to rest at least part of their case on the supposition of Hanoi's willingness to negotiate and had to discredit the sincerity of the U.S.'s own offer. The path led into a thicket of diplomatic details where the public was hardly apt to follow.

The second event was the American intervention in the Dominican Republic. It demonstrated the government's willingness to undertake the same sort of action again which had previously led to the morass in Vietnam. Suddenly, the focus of the debate shifted from the single case of Vietnam to U.S. foreign policy in its entirety. The revolutionist approach gained adherents rapidly. A few Christians, particularly concerned about American policy in Latin America, began to believe that only a Vietcong victory in Southeast Asia could force a radical change in American foreign policy.

Escalation continued. The Churches began to respond officially. In December, 1965, the General Assembly of the National Council of Churches called for a negotiated settlement which would free "South Vietnam from outside interference, with complete liberty to determine the character of its future government by the result of a peaceful, free and verified choice of its people". It asked the U.S. to agree to "a phased withdrawal of all its troops and bases from the Vietnamese territory, if and when they can be replaced by adequate international peacekeeping forces". The same proposals were made a month later in a policy statement of the Synagogue Council of America. Neither statement offered a direct condemnation of American policy; but appearing in the context of the government's insistence that all steps toward peace were being taken, they had the character of criticism.

The Catholic Bishops issued a Pastoral Statement on Peace and Vietnam the next November (1966). It was even milder than the Protestant or Jewish statements and, in fact, explicitly supported the war: "We can conscientiously support the position

of our country in the present circumstances." The Pastoral Statement did stress personal responsibility in scrutinizing the morality of the war, and it called attention to the moral limitations on
all warfare. "It is the duty of everyone to search for other alter-
natives. And everyone—Government leaders and citizens alike
—must be prepared to change our course whenever a change in
circumstances warrants it. . . . And we must clearly protest
whenever there is a danger that the conflict will be escalated beyond morally acceptable limits." Once again, the context was
crucial: for the traditionally anti-Communist Catholic hierarchy
to emphasize these hesitations in time of war was notable. Yet
the language was general and abstract; if the moment were to
come when Catholics could no longer "conscientiously support"
their country, would it be identifiable by anything in the Bishops'
statement? One is reminded of Camus' complaint: "What the
world expects of Christians is that Christians should speak out
loud and clear. . . . They should get away from abstraction
and confront the blood-stained face history has taken on today."

Twenty-five hundred Christian and Jewish clergymen consciously tried to meet Camus' challenge when they drafted a
statement on the war at a Washington meeting in January of
1967. They protested "the immorality of the warfare in Vietnam
. . . in which civilian casualties are greater than military . . .
in which the widespread use of napalm and other explosives is
killing and maiming women, children, and the aged. . . . Our
ongoing escalation, far from bringing the war closer to an end,
serves rather to increase its duration and intensity. . . ."

The Catholic lay-edited weekly *Commonweal* declared in its
December 23, 1966 issue: "The United States should get out
of Vietnam . . . even at the cost of a Communist victory. . . .
The war in Vietnam is an unjust one . . . what is being done
there, despite the almost certain good intentions of those doing
it, is a crime and a sin." Perhaps most striking was the protest
raised by *Christianity and Crisis,* a Protestant journal founded
in 1941 to *combat* American isolationism and well-known for
its recognition of the unavoidable ambiguities of all political

problems. In March of 1966 its Editorial Board declared the war in Vietnam "destructive to the people whom we claim to be helping, to the peace of the world, and to our best interests". The positions taken by these two journals mark the shift among significant Christian advocates of an internationalist-realist approach from censure of many of the means of war used in Vietnam to an outright condemnation of the war as unjust.

The appearance of Martin Luther King in the ranks of the anti-war protesters in April of 1967 may have marked another phase in the Vietnam debate. King is basically a pacifist, and it is clear that his remarks are a mixture of every possible objection to the war. Growing more desperate as the war continues and enlarges, protesters are less concerned with intellectual consistency than with mobilizing various sections of the population (Negroes, poor people, students, religious groups) into united opposition.

These voices of opposition may be impressive, but it must be recognized that the vast majority of American Christians support the war. A few do so enthusiastically, and their position has been summed up in the sarcastic anti-war slogan, "Kill a Commie for Christ!" Most, however, accept the war as a grim duty—but a *moral* one. To have the ability to prevent another Communist regime and not to do so would be an abdication of moral responsibility.

Yet Americans are profoundly disturbed by the war in Vietnam. There is little surprise in this. Not only are the military virtues not prized in America, but more important the horrors of a distant war have seldom been communicated to a home population in such terrifying clarity. If American mass media have frequently accepted the government's word on the diplomatic aspects of the war, they have nonetheless pictured fully the sheer destruction, the burnt and torn bodies of Vietnamese children, the demoralization of Vietnamese society. Polls of American opinion show that most Americans expect the war to end in a "compromise settlement" and not a "clear-cut victory", and they are willing to abide by this result.

But no Communist regime—that is the moral imperative which is ultimately determining. As long as the government can convince Americans that a given action is absolutely necessary to prevent this outcome, they appear willing to assent. Concessions are possible, but only to a point. Escalation, "if necessary", is virtually open-ended.

All talk of negotiations, settlements, or withdrawal must eventually confront the fact of anti-Communism. Despite the $1 billion in aid the U.S. has given Yugoslavia, anti-Communism remains an absolute in the public's view of foreign policy. To that extent, it has become an idol. The first business of the Churches, one would think, is to preach against idols. But against this idol they have not preached. Indeed they have frequently encouraged its cult. The Churches must face the issue squarely and speak clearly and simply: "To raise opposition to Communism to an absolute in whose name all can be done is to offer blood sacrifice before a false god."

François Lepargneur, O.P. / *São Paulo, Brazil*

The Christian Conscience of Brazil

Underdevelopment in today's world represents an obstacle to the formation of solidarity between nations on a Christian or a truly human level. It is a sign of our failure to achieve this goal. We need only point to the fact that most of the developed nations have refused to contribute 1% of their national revenue to the underdeveloped nations, and that the gap between rich and poor nations is steadily widening. Here we should like to focus on the internal problems of one developing nation, Brazil.

Low per capita income, meager industrialization and widespread illiteracy have existed for centuries, but the question of underdevelopment has only come to the fore in recent times. It becomes an issue when the outlook of the developed nations takes hold in countries that have not developed their natural resources (or have developed them mainly for some colonial ruler), *when these countries are suddenly called upon to accomplish in a few decades what European nations have achieved over the past century or two.* The problem of underdevelopment is one result of the growth of a worldwide human culture, and it is further aggravated by a variety of circumstances: in Brazil, for example, by the astounding growth of the population rate.

The Traditional Outlook

Let us try to situate the Christian conscience within the context of the general situation in Brazil. To understand the present-day situation, we must look back at the past and forward toward the demands of the near future. For a long time the outlook of many Brazilian Catholics has been that of a counter-reformation Christianity, and it still is. Counter-reformation theology has shaped this outlook. The Christian conscience in Brazil is *pleased with itself,* and *obedience* is the basic virtue on which the social structure is built. The faithful must put their wholehearted trust in God and his providence; and he speaks to them through historical events and through civil and religious authorities, who "know" his mind and serve as his spokesmen. The inevitable tensions that arise between these two seats of authority are resolved by compromise and accommodation at the top levels. In the light of historical conditions, the Church represents continuity, uniformity and the absolute vis-à-vis a civil government that is subject to the changing winds of palace revolts. "Sacred" means immovable.

In such a situation love of God takes precedence over love for mankind—to say the least. And love of neighbor means teaching him to give thanks to God, to turn his eyes heavenward and to obey the established order. A man is happy to the extent that he has learned the lesson of *Christian resignation:* one must "conform", one must submit to God's will by accepting the capricious whims of nature, the Church and the established power structure.

"Are you a believer?" That question does not even come up in Brazil. An affirmative answer is presumed by the very fact of your nationality, and social pressure maintains this faith among the various classes. Man is a creature and a subject; in other words, he is passive and obedient. Any new problem that might crop up will be solved by the leaders of Church and State.

Earth-Shaking New Forces

The modern world is breaking in upon this universe with all the fury of a cyclone. Urbanization, industrialization, the new stress on education, the new methods of science, man's new historical awareness and his quest for individual freedom—all these forces are challenging the vestiges of feudalism that still remain, and also have repercussions in the religious sphere. People now see a temporal order where religious salvation is bound up with man's advancement in history. The individual conscience confronts questions it cannot leave to the hierarchy. Certain options now become a matter for personal decisions.

People are discovering that the traditional outlook took a fatalistic view toward the human condition and did little to advance the cause of social progress. *A new concern for man's condition in the world* is taking hold, and this is an important turn of events. Poverty, exploitation of the weak by the strong and the whole web of natural and social restraints are no longer regarded as inevitable conditions that embody an inscrutable and unchangeable divine plan.

Some have come to realize that the keystone of Christian ethics is not obedience but charity. During the past centuries charity had been buried within the people's natural religious spirit, but now it summons all to focus on the concrete dictates of the second great commandment. Christian love, to be sure, has always focused on man. But its stress on the dignity of man usually referred to his transcendence and his supernatural vocation. The salvation of the individual was the thing that had to be secured; the moral code and the sacramental system were the means employed.

In this framework, social classes and structures did not come into question. Quite the contrary: the religious aura surrounding them forced the individual to accept them for the sake of his salvation. The harsh drawbacks of these structures were ameliorated by individual initiative and the efforts of religious orders. But the individual found himself enclosed within a system that vigorously repulsed any threat from within or from without. The only avenue of escape was the realm of spiritual realities. The social values and the ideas of personal advancement that we advocate today remained eschatological promises, signposts of a world beyond.

Many historical factors have helped to undermine this world view. Democracy introduced the notion that the lower echelons should have some say in formulating the law of society; and to make this contribution, they were entitled to acquire the necessary information. The advancement of science reinforced this burgeoning self-awareness, adding a canon of required criteria. By this time the emphasis on individual judgment had wiped out the possibility of unanimity, which once had been ensured by authoritative institutions. In the 19th century various Protestant groups spread through the land, with Bible in hand. In the 20th century practical atheism is spreading in the large cities. Today we find that among the middle class and the students a Christian conscience can no longer coexist with a Christian Weltanschauung; one's religious life is a personal matter; Mass attendance does not preclude contempt for the progress of civilization; the nation is not going to collapse if the Church loses its hold on individual consciences.

Vatican Council II accelerated this whole process. It confirmed the outlook of those forward-looking people who felt that certain distinctions had to be made. These people, however, were afraid to speak up on their own, because their views would disturb others whose outlook was based on the permanence of the Church's tradition and who used this to justify the most extreme forms of conservatism in social matters.

And indeed the Christian conscience of Brazil does not yet correspond to the outlook of Vatican Council II. People's minds cannot be changed right away, because many social and cultural factors stand in the way. Most priests were molded in seminaries where the spirit of Trent and Vatican I held sway. They were ill prepared for dialogue. Their theology courses were comprised of defined canons and conciliar anathemas, or at best, of paraphrased versions of Pius XII's encyclicals.

Certain tensions are now coming to light, e.g., between the natural religious spirit of the people and the external formalism of dogma, between their ready spirit of tolerance and the intolerance of their Church. Now that the Council has come and gone, the clergy accepts the notion of ecumenism as something approved by the Church to stem the spread of sectarianism and syncretism. The Catholic hierarchy has been taken by surprise by an evolutionary change that is moving much too fast for it. Accepting the Council's decisions in principle, it finds itself in an embarrassing position when it thinks through all the practical consequences of these decisions. It has turned to the problem of development with remarkable suddenness, but it is still wary about the notion of lay participation.

These limitations are understandable within the overall Brazilian context, but that does not make them any less problematical. Apropos of *development,* the question of civil liberties is linked up historically with that of democratic progress. But few bishops would accept the notion that the faithful could challenge the restrictions placed on individual liberty by the State.

As far as freedom of *information* is concerned, Catholic organisms (rarely in the hands of the laity) bear witness more to the lack of cultural progress than to any easing of censure. At the same time, the professional press (which is not guided by the tenets of faith) continues to serve the interests of privileged capitalists while claiming to be defending the values of "Christian civilization".

The Acid Test Today

The *Christian conscience,* however, is ceasing to be an institutional reality and is evolving into a personal attribute—among the educated, at least. But this too is creating difficulties. The current problems that confront the European conscience are reaching the laity of Brazil at a time when the old authoritarian solutions no longer satisfy them, and when the hierarchy has not yet managed to work up a satisfactory new approach. An age-old shallowness, which once went unnoticed, is now being seen clearly; there are no constructive, pastoral-minded theologians to enlighten the new Christian conscience. People are still unwilling to face the hard fact that it is Brazil's elite, not her poverty-stricken masses, that are turning away from the faith.

When society lived a stable existence, problems cropped up gradually and the stress on obedience led people to accept the answers handed down by the hierarchy. The problems of the past did not have so many technical aspects as those of the present day. Thus the old political relationship worked well. The government hierarchy and the ecclesiastical hierarchy got together and worked out a diplomatic solution (that was the type of dialogue that took place between the Church and the world), or else the local bishop settled the question.

Present-day problems of conscience have repercussions on the Christian conscience, and they cannot be restrained within the old framework of relationships. One begins to see how useful it would be for the hierarchy to have its own body of experts, competent in the various fields of human knowledge.

In Latin America, everybody claims to know what Christianity is. That shows how important words are, and how inadequate. We must have other signs to prove that the Church is interested in human beings, not just in herself. To put it another way, *it is the question of development that provides us with concrete criteria for judging the authenticity of the Christian conscience today.* It is not enough to proclaim the lofty dignity of the human person; we must respect men's consciences within the framework of ecclesial society. After all, we judge a seed by the fruit it bears.

If Christian eschatology leaves the temporal incarnation of its values for the end of time, it is proclaiming its disinterest in history. Moreover, everyone claims to be a defender of man and his authentic liberty. The future of the Christian conscience in Latin America, of its authenticity and its diffusion, depends less on the orthodoxy of its ideas than on the effectiveness of its influence.

Considering the past and present influence of the Church in

Latin America, the hierarchy cannot opt out of the question of social, economic and political evolution on the grounds that that is not its domain. It cannot disclaim responsibility for the past, nor disown a large measure of responsibility for what is going on today. No one expects the hierarchy to accomplish the task of development by itself, but it is responsible for development in that its task is to form the Christian conscience of its people.

Martin Ekwa, S.J./*Kinshasa, Congo*

Racism in Central and South Africa

From the beginning of Israel's history her biblical sages spoke of the grandeur and dignity of man. Created in God's image, men shared a common origin and were equal to one another. When Christ came, he spoke to men of their common destiny and of God's plan to gather all nations into the unity of a single family. On the eve of his death Christ bequeathed the gift of peace to his disciples, and he offered this prayer to his Father: "Keep in thy name those whom thou hast given to me, that they may be one even as we are." [1]

The Grandeur of Man

This was the extraordinary message that flickered within the bosom of the great empires of those bygone days. Was it not the inspiration for the great declarations of our day concerning the rights of man?

However, a sublime message and its inspiring corollaries are not enough to ensure that men will come to each other's aid or that nations will collaborate as brothers for their mutual progress. As Pope John XXIII pointed out in *Pacem in terris,* interpersonal and international relations pose complex and delicate questions. And to solve them, government leaders must possess balanced judgment, moral integrity, profound insight and com-

[1] Jn. 17, 11.

71

mon sense. Solutions will come only when all men base their actions on truth, justice and charity.

A person can change the world and the hearts of men only if
he has faith in man's potentialities for good, only if he is convinced his creative determination can mold something worthwhile in the furnace of day-to-day activity.

What is charity, after all? Is it not keeping one's eyes and
ears open to the world's crying needs, knowing how to help
others without depriving them of their proper responsibility, as-
sisting without dictating, serving without enslaving? Is it not
showing consideration, respect and understanding for others, be
they persons, nations or races? With such an attitude man establishes an authentic relationship with others, a relationship that
gives rise to varied forms of assistance and fruitful activities. As
Pope Paul VI said at the United Nations: "Peace . . . is built
with the mind, with ideas, with the works of peace . . . this is
your essential task . . . this is the finest aspect of the United
Nations Organization, its very genuine human side . . . the reflection of the plan of God." [2] This is one of the objectives behind
God's act of creation: the creation of a united human race,
pulsing with one heart and bound together by love.

The Courage to Love

God's aim to establish peace and unity among men is also our
vocation as individuals. But love calls for constant conquest over
the self and often demands great courage. This is the price which
must be paid to awaken and foster the spirit of trust that paves
the way for true dialogue and effective cooperation. This courage
is even more necessary when personal differences are involved.
Each person has his own life history and his own scale of values;
to harmonize the varied threads of different lives is a delicate
operation. Even when the possibilities for harmony seem closer
at hand, communal life can be made quite difficult by forgetful-
ness, insincerity, unreasonableness or reproaches. This holds true
for interpersonal relations, and it also holds true for relations

[2] Paul VI, Address to U.N. General Assembly, October 4, 1965.

between nation and nation and relations between a nation and the whole world community. The actions of men have a greater impact on these relationships than do impersonal economic and political forces.

The Plague of Racism

Over against this stirring panorama of a world drawing closer together stands the menace of racism. It has assumed worldwide proportions, sowing the poisonous seeds of hate everywhere and outshadowing any physical or economic evil.

Racism is one of the dangers that threaten world peace. It is one of those topics that nice people do not talk about. Yet, at this writing, the African press headlines the story of a 55-nation meeting at Dar-Es-Salaam, where the deleterious effects of racism (on Africa and the whole world) will be discussed.

Racism is the plague of our times. And, unfortunately, its victims often see no other means of combatting it than to fight fire with fire. Black racism becomes the defense against white racism. As Berdyaev put it: "The fight against evil often becomes an evil itself . . . to overcome evil, good people turn into evildoers and return evil for evil." [3]

Racism has often sought to justify itself on rational grounds. There are, for example, the theories of men like Gobineau and Hitler. Others will weave fantastic arguments out of Sacred Scripture to prove the evil nature of the race of Ham. Having proved the congenital inferiority of a given race, it can proclaim the superiority of another race and justify the suppression of the inferior one. Racist doctrines are the product of human pride and human arrogance. It is easy to see why the Church has condemned them on more than one occasion. As the Conference of South African Bishops declared in July, 1957: "It is a sin to debase one's fellow man."

Racism has been condemned by the popes and by the recent Council. The Christian concept of man is diametrically opposed

[3] Nikolai Berdyaev, *The Divine and the Human* (London: G. Bles, 1949).

to that of racism. Indeed, the racist view of man is contrary to the very essence of Christianity. Racism is not only a crime and a sin, it is also a heresy. A person can commit sins and remain a Christian. He has a right, as it were, to be weak, to be a "sinner". But he cannot reject the very essence of Christianity and remain a Christian!

The racism of the emerging nations, however, is not a dogmatic racism. It is rather a psycho-social phenomenon that manifests itself in aggression: civil disorders and tribal warfare. On January 4, 1959, riots broke out in Kinshasa; they came as suddenly and as unexpectedly as a tropical storm. Their purpose was to shake up the colonial regime. Proper names disappeared and people were labelled by their color: white man, black man. The victims of such disorders are usually not the white people, and those white people who are attacked are usually those who fraternize with black people. One such white man was knocked off his motorcycle as he was returning from a visit to a sick Negro friend. His white skin labelled him an enemy.

This type of racism is an act of self-defense against the stranger, the person who is unlucky enough to be different from oneself. To satisfy its thirst for power, influence and control, a group will set itself up as superior to some other group. This psycho-social brand of racism, the defensive gesture of a frightened person, is found in varying degrees throughout the world. Indeed the whole notion of the "inferiority complex" may provide much of the psychological explanation for racism. The frightened person shuts himself up within his own group, arms himself, tries to hold onto the ground he has gained and the material advantages he has acquired, and creates ghettoes with their stifling atmosphere.

This spontaneous racism has spread instinctively throughout the world. In Africa it has struck deep roots and blossomed into a gigantic tree, casting its dark shadows everywhere. For several centuries the Negro race has been the chosen victim. Docile and submissive to the "superior race", it has known the slave trade, colonization and the color bar. Politically and economically the

Negro has been treated as an irresponsible minor. He has lived as an outcast in society. His culture has been put down as one of the exotic plants of the world, a primitive and infantile thing. The color of his skin is the criterion by which he is judged.

The person who has never suffered the ravages of racial discrimination cannot easily appreciate its effects on an individual or a race. Few have tried to answer the question that Griffin[4] asked himself: "How does a person feel when he is subjected to discriminatory measures because of the color of his skin, something over which he has no control?" Griffin had his skin dyed black, and for six weeks he lived the life of a Negro. He closes his book with this prayer: "I pray God that the Negro will not waste his opportunities to build a better life for himself, to use the strength he has gained from his sufferings without descending to vengeance."

In his flesh and his heart the black man bears the scars of racial discrimination. Remember the day Peter Abrahams[5] went for a walk: "I went to use the public rest room only to find this notice over all the toilets—WHITES ONLY. I went to sit down on a park bench, only to find the same notice—WHITES ONLY. I was an intruder, and so I took to my heels furtively."

One day a white friend of mine said: "South Africa is a special case." Of course it is! So is the United States, so is everywhere else! Every case is special. But they do share a common feature: they all show "disregard for the dignity of the human person". We find stores, hospitals, movie houses and schools that are for whites only. Sometimes the separation between the races is so complete that we seem to be facing an impregnable barrier that will never be toppled. For the Negro, his race seems to be his badge of shame, a badge that can never be discarded.

Is "shame" too strong a word? Read the works of certain ethnologists. The Negro race is put on display, clinically dissected by amateur psychologists who refuse to give serious con-

[4] John Howard Griffin, *Black Like Me* (Boston: Houghton Mifflin, 1961).
[5] Peter Abrahams, *Tell Freedom* (New York: Alfred A. Knopf, 1954).

sideration to the deeper personality of the black man. They do not notice the reserve and the ashamed look of an underprivileged person, but they do notice the crop of his hair, the length of his nails and the thickness of his lips. These somatic characteristics provide the premises for a time-worn syllogism, one which concludes that the Negro race is inferior. As Emile Faguet put it: "The 'Barbarians', after all, belong to the same race as the Greeks and Romans; they are cousins. The yellow and the black races are not our cousins at all. There is a marked difference and a great distance between them and us, ethnologically speaking."

We have moved far beyond Faguet, of course, but how many people still feel the same way even though they do not express it openly? Even though nothing is said, the Negro suffers humiliation. He has felt the inhuman and barbaric lash of racial discrimination. It is time for Christians and all men of goodwill to face the truth, as Paul VI spelled it out in his encyclical *Populorum progressio;* instead, many people regard racism as a problem of private morality, a problem posed by the Negro himself who suffers from an inferiority complex and refuses to see himself as he really is! Someone must be mistaken in this sad affair . . . Yet it is the voice of racism's victims that has pointed out the honorable road, the voice of a Martin Luther King or a Franz Fanon.

The Only Remedy

At this point the reader is probably inclined to say that it is not enough to diagnose the malady and condemn it, that one must also suggest a cure. Well, the cure will not come from the psychologist, the psychiatrist, the anthropologist, the legislator or the law officer. The only remedies for racism are charity, sympathy, communion and respect for others. The sacred value of the human person transcends his physical characteristics or his racial type. A little love will cure us of racism and transform our ideas, our opinions and our day-to-day behavior.

All men share the same feelings and the same sufferings. Sorrow plagues men in every part of the world. Who would stop to wonder about the color of their skin? If men love and suffer the same way, should they not be able to deal lovingly and magnanimously with each other without any thought of racial distinctions?

In our day, when nations are getting together more and more, the call to charity has taken on new dimensions in the personal and international sphere. If Christians remain faithful to their master's message of peace and unity, racism will give way to the God-given gift of love.

Paul-Marcel Lemaire, O.P./*Montreal, Canada*

French Canada: A Challenge
to the Christian Conscience

A study of the Church in French Canada must take into account both the Christian and the secular situation. This Church is said to be going through a severe crisis because it is in an awkward position between two spheres.

Most observers tend to define the Church in relation to some other body. They criticize its internal mechanisms by referring to external criteria, viz., those of the secular society; and to make things easier, they suppose that everything in society is running beautifully. It is of course very difficult to speak of the Church without reference to the society in which it is placed. The Church is very much a part of that society and most citizens of Quebec find it quite natural (too natural perhaps) to belong to two communities. This comparative method is in danger of isolating the two spheres and forgetting (as the sociologist Fernand Dumont recently pointed out) that a similar and related crisis is occurring in both the religious and the secular sphere, and that theological criteria are also valuable in any attempt at analysis.

The secular and the religious spheres, as terms of the discussion, must themselves be examined. Is it true that the French Canadian Church has existed in the past in a Christian *milieu?* The reply to this question cannot be a straightforward one, and first, of course, the term Christian must be clarified. This

"Christianity" has done little theorizing about the relation between the ecclesiastical and the civil sphere. Since the British
conquest in 1760 and British influenced governments thereafter,
there has been no systematic cooperation between the two powers.
The Church, having gained numerous civil benefits, tended to
behave like any other large institution; officialdom, often impersonal, paternalist or authoritarian, set limits on cultural
creativity. From the beginning of the century up to the present
time the Church's ideology was nationalistic and the faith inseparable from the French language.

And what of secularization about which so much is said? If
the word is used to mean that process by which the external
presence of religion is less and less in evidence in daily life,
then it is true that it affects the mass of Christians whether they
realize it or not. This withdrawal of religion from daily life is
not usually explained in terms of the distinction between the
sacred and the secular. There is work here for the Christian
conscience, even though it may not want to identify its relationship with God and its attitude to the "sacred sphere" or to see
the secular as a world closed in on itself. For at the moment
the world confronts the Christian as it confronts the young
child, as the delicious place which arouses countless uncertain
desires. Daily life, and especially public life, is not subjected to
the Gospel or even to non-religious moral considerations. In
this sense human life is not secularized enough to *become*
authentically Christian. Religion is a support or a safeguard
only in very limited spheres of private life.

This leads us to say a few words about life in Quebec at the
moment, sociologically speaking. French Canada is far more
Americanized than it realizes. American culture is becoming a
universal phenomenon and its characteristics are well known:
the importance given to an immediate return, obsession with
comfort, confidence in, and passive acceptance of, public opinion, an alarming lack of critical spirit, gregarianism and con-
formism both in the "peer groups" of adolescence and in adult
society.

The rapid urbanization of the country and the "peaceful revolution" of 1960 have contributed, in this general framework, to considerable changes in Quebec society. The growing division between public and private life gives rise to new attitudes, toward the family and leisure, for example. Social life has taken on new forms, friends replacing the family group. And a new nationalism has emerged, which is eager to break with the past and build a socialist Quebec.

Christianity has contributed very little to these events and often gives the impression, particularly to the young, that its importance in this new world is a very marginal one. There are very few adult Christians who have patently and successfully reconciled this new society with their faith. If there is a crisis in the Church in Quebec, it is not because it is not properly structured to cope with the challenge of this changing society (society is changing in every country in the world), but because her own members have not assimilated the Gospel in a way that would make it a transforming influence in daily life. The crisis is not primarily at the sociological or official level but at the level of faith, both private and collective. There is a gap between the faith instinct which is often still strong, and the understanding of the faith, which has not been formulated in a language fit to deal with these present needs. This is not of course an entirely new problem, but it has become so acute, particularly among the young, that their faith instinct is in danger of disappearing altogether for lack of the language.

What is the reaction of Catholics and in particular of the clergy to this situation? They are worried chiefly about three problems, internal pastoral matters, religious education and the general cultural influence of religion. There is quite a lot of disagreement on all these matters. There is much confusion in thought and groping in action.

The renewal in catechesis, liturgy and preaching has only been going on for about ten years. Nevertheless there are people ready to accuse this renewal of selling out to an easy secularization and to recommend the Church to concentrate on missionary activity toward the lapsed. This is a misunderstanding. Doesn't the rate of lapsing suggest rather that the internal reform of the Church should be carried further rather than held up? Bad preaching, untidy and depressing liturgical assemblies exasperate the faithful. Parochial practice, which has enormous problems to face, such as putting its enormous churches to proper use, is lacking in imagination and prudent initiative.

But it is the human set-up which needs changing. The laity complain of authoritarianism and too impersonal relationships between them and the clergy. They do not formulate their discontent very clearly but they want radical changes in these matters. Everyone is now talking about dialogue, but a true dialogue is often lacking even between clergy and laity. The true spirit of the Gospel would be better promoted by a more democratic structure and by working and communicating in ways more like the modern methods in education.

An analysis of the religious crisis discloses an acute need for better religious education. However, many priests are misled by a false activism and the demands of shorter term requirements and overlook the need for better education. Under the pretext of being in touch with daily life, they often give very "small beer" in their preaching and catechesis and their ancient anti-intellectual bias makes them suspicious of theology.

All sociological surveys have revealed that the mass of Christians live by a very impoverished form of belief. Their faith, even the faith of educated persons, is often seriously disturbed by modern forms of idolatry, scientific discoveries or simply by their impatient demand for social emancipation. The evangelization of intelligence is therefore of the utmost importance in order to make it more critical of the modern way of life. Even though this is a French-speaking people, they have not absorbed at all adequately the great French critical tradition; they are not ready enough to question what they see and hear.

Religious education must place faith firmly on the basis of the kerygma and show the originality of Christianity without sociologizing or moralizing reductionism. This renewed faith will require a renewed spirituality. The absence of prayer in Christian life is quite alarming and needs something to be done about it. This new spirituality would probably be theological rather than emotional, missionary rather than devotional, and its attitude to the world would be inquiring before it was proselytizing.

The problem of the general cultural influence of the Church is also a difficult one. In the past the Church took it upon itself to provide schools, hospitals, welfare, and this tradition is still active in the Christian conscience. But now the State is assuming its own responsibilities and wishes to mobilize all its resources in the provision of government facilities. And Catholics are confused about whether their support is due to the ecclesiastical on the state schemes.

There is a tendency to confine the Christian role in the world to the welfare sphere and forget the mission to proclaim the Gospel. There is a danger that the transcendent aspect of Christianity will be ignored. This we think may be a sign of nostalgia for the faith in those who have formally abandoned it. Must Christians justify their beliefs by competing with non-Christians in the transformation of the world? Is his contribution to social problems the only thing the priest has to give the world?

Of course Catholics must be actively concerned with social problems. They are confronted by a major challenge. But it is an ambivalent challenge. Is their Christian hope to rest in their success in solving social problems? If so they will be bitterly disappointed. How can they both commit themselves to the needs of this world while preserving the freedom and inner values of the Gospel?

Christians are reluctant to leave social problems entirely to the secular arm. They want to find a role for the Church, to disturb consciences, to arouse enthusiasm, to witness to spiritual and personal values not reducible to a purely material conception of human existence. In this way Catholics could be active in the world and give proof of their goodwill and love for all their human brothers. This would not of course prevent them from engaging in purely Catholic enterprises.

This course is only followed by a minority. The rest drift indifferently and are not in the least concerned by the purely formal presence of the Church in countless organizations. There are Catholics and even priests who simply give up the attempt to bear witness to the Gospel in the world. Others, in fact most others, opt for ghetto politics and clumsy defenses of the "rights of the Church" in the world. This leaves the Church far behind.

A conception of the Church as the leaven of the world, servant of Christ and of men, free to act in the service of the Gospel is not the conception in every Christian conscience. But there are signs of renewal, particularly in certain active religious communities.

William Hamilton/*Rochester, N. Y.*

A Note on Radical Theology

1. *A Radical Quotation*

Thanksgiving Day came and went without any fuss while Yossarian was still in the hospital. The only bad thing about it was the turkey for dinner, and even that was pretty good. It was the most rational Thanksgiving he had ever spent, and he took a sacred oath to spend every future Thanksgiving Day in the cloistered shelter of a hospital. He broke his sacred oath the very next year, when he spent the holiday in a hotel room instead in intellectual conversation with Lieutenant Scheisskopf's wife, who had Dori Duz's dog tags on for the occasion and who henpecked Yossarian sententiously for being cynical and callous about Thanksgiving, even though she didn't believe in God just as much as he didn't.

"I'm probably just as good an atheist as you are," she speculated boastfully. "But even I feel that we all have a great deal to be thankful for and that we shouldn't be ashamed to show it."

"Name one thing I've got to be thankful for," Yossarian challenged her without interest.

"Well . . ." Lieutenant Scheisskopf's wife mused and paused a moment to ponder dubiously. "Me."

"Oh, come on," he scoffed.

She arched her eyebrows in surprise. "Aren't you thankful for me?" she asked. She frowned peevishly, her pride wounded. "I don't have to shack up with you, you know," she told him with cold dignity. "My husband has a whole squadron full of aviation cadets who would be only too happy to shack up with their commanding officer's wife just for the added fillip it would give them."

Yossarian decided to change the subject. "Now you're changing the subject," he pointed out diplomatically. "I'll bet I can name two things to be miserable about for every one you can name to be thankful for."

"Be thankful you've got me," she insisted.

"I am, honey. But I'm also goddam good and miserable that I can't have Dori Duz again, too. Or the hundreds of other girls and women I'll see and want in my short lifetime and won't be able to go to bed with even once."

"Be thankful you're healthy."

"Be bitter you're not going to stay that way."

"Be glad you're even alive."

"Be furious you're going to die."

"Things could be much worse," she cried.

"They could be one hell of a lot better," he answered heatedly.

"You're naming only one thing," she protested. "You said you could name two."

"And don't tell me God works in mysterious ways," Yossarian continued, hurtling on over her objection. "There's nothing so mysterious about it. He's not working at all. He's playing. Or else He's forgotten all about us. That's the kind of God you people talk about—a countrybumpkin, a clumsy, bungling, brainless, conceited, uncouth hayseed. Good God, how much reverence can you have for a Supreme Being who finds it necessary to include such phenomena as phlegm and tooth decay in His divine system of creation? What in the world was running through that warped, evil, scatalogical mind of His when He robbed old people of the power to control their bowel movements? Why in the world did He ever create pain?"

"*Pain?*" *Lieutenant Scheisskopf's wife pounced upon the word victoriously. "Pain is a useful symptom. Pain is a warning to us of bodily dangers."*

"*And who created the dangers?*" *Yossarian demanded. He laughed caustically. "Oh, He was really being charitable to us when He gave us pain! Why couldn't He have used a doorbell instead to notify us, or one of his celestial choirs? Or a system of blue-and-red neon tubes right in the middle of each person's forehead. Any jukebox manufacturer worth his salt could have done that. Why couldn't He?*"

"*People would certainly look silly walking around with red neon tubes in the middle of their foreheads.*"

"*They certainly look beautiful now writhing in agony or stupefied with morphine, don't they? What a colossal, immortal blunderer! When you consider the opportunity and power He had to really do a job, and then look at the stupid, ugly little mess He made of it instead, His sheer incompetence is almost staggering. It's obvious He never met a payroll. Why, no self-respecting businessman would hire a bungler like Him as even a shipping clerk!*"

Lieutenant Scheisskopf's wife had turned ashen in disbelief and was ogling him with alarm. "You'd better not talk that way about Him, honey," she warned him reprovingly in a low and hostile voice. "He might punish you."

"*Isn't He punishing me enough?*" *Yossarian snorted resentfully. "You know, we mustn't let Him get away with it. Oh, no, we certainly mustn't let Him get away scot free for all the sorrow He's caused us. Someday I'm going to make Him pay. I know when. On the Judgment Day. Yes, that's the day I'll be close enough to reach out and grab that little yokel by His neck and—*"

"*Stop it! Stop it!*" *Lieutenant Scheisskopf's wife screamed suddenly, and began beating him ineffectually about the head with both fists. "Stop it!"*

Yossarian ducked behind his arm for protection while she

slammed away at him in feminine fury for a few seconds, and then he caught her determinedly by the wrists and forced her gently back down on the bed. "What the hell are you getting so upset about?" he asked her bewilderedly in a tone of contrite amusement. "I thought you didn't believe in God."

"I don't," she sobbed, bursting violently into tears. "But the God I don't believe in is a good God, a just God, a merciful God. He's not the mean and stupid God you make Him out to be."

Yossarian laughed and turned her arms loose. "Let's have a little more religious freedom between us," he proposed obligingly. "You don't believe in the God you want to, and I won't believe in the God I want to. Is that a deal?"

Joseph Heller, *Catch 22*, pp. 183-185

2. *What Does Radical Theology Mean?*

The "death of God" or radical theology is two things, one past, one present. It *was* a journalistic pseudo-event which took place sometime between October 1965 and April 1966, largely in the United States. This event made a large splash; it was enjoyed by some, regretted by others, upset a few and—among other things—elicited some quite idiotic statements from ordinarily sage and loving spirits such as Reinhold Niebuhr.

But that is over, that part of the event, and radical theology has not gone away. For radical theology was also—and still is —a rather small movement in American Protestant theology which began in the late 1950's, and which brought together a number of thinkers who could not do their work either with Barth's archaism, Bultmann's demythologizing, Tillich's correlation, or Bonhoeffer's non-religious interpretation. But each of these great men made an important, if inadvertent, contribution to the radical mood and movement.

It remains to be seen if radical theology is more than "mood and movement". It clearly has been a catalyst, bringing the forgotten doctrine of God back to the center, but its historical, systematic and ethical work is largely ahead of it. If one asked for a sentence-answer to the question, what are you doing, radical theology would probably answer: "We are trying to see if it is possible to live and think as a Christian without God, and we see this experiment as both a practical-political and theoretical-theological task."

3. *A Religious Revolution in Three Ages*

But before we turn to clarify this "answer", it might be appropriate to step back a moment from the radical theology and even from Protestantism in particular. For there is, at least in that part of Christendom represented by Western Europe and the North American continent, a palpable religious revolution going on, and radical theology and all the other highly publicized religious events and pseudo-events must be understood against the background of this revolution. Is there any way of defining this revolution? Can a revolution ever be defined, or do we just have to live with it: to get with it or to reject it? I would like to try to propose a conceptual scheme by which this revolution can be understood. For if we don't try to do something like this, we are at the mercy of the under-educated journalists and the threatened religious leaders for both our data and our responses.

I don't think the Reformation is a helpful model for the revolution we are in. It is, in fact, as unhelpful religiously as Munich is politically when used as an event to justify America's immoral continuation of the Vietnamese destruction. For the Reformation, oddly enough, was a decisive and fast-moving thing. One could point to dates, times and persons. This is not the case with our religious revolution (though if any document could possibly be the 95 theses of our revolution, it would almost certainly be Bonhoeffer's prison letters). What is happening to us is actually more like the Renaissance, which was recently defined as an attempt to find a compromise formula (*Ausgleichs-formel*) for those who wished to live with Christian convictions and classical forms. Our revolution has a similar problem: the attempt to find a means whereby one may live in one's religious place as a fully contemporary man or woman.

Let me propose a scheme that may help us see what is going on. I take it that we can understand the Western religious tradition in terms of three ages, three periods.

We may provisionally and roughly date *the first age* from Abraham to Luther, and we may say that its main problem was the naming of God—Who art Thou? This is the time of the Jewish-Christian tradition, the classical Christian era. The monuments and works of this age are simple to state: Catholicism, Scripture, Chartres, the Divine Comedy, the saint.

The second age, from Luther to Freud or perhaps Sartre, has another main problem. Not the naming of the gods, but the naming of the self. Not the look upwards (Gothic) but the look within. "Who am I?" This age has also familiar characteristics: Protestantism, the hero, the explorer, bourgeois man, self and identity problems, pietism, experience, psychoanalysis, existentialism, goals, values, the performance principle.

And *the third age,* from Freud or Sartre, from yesterday or today to—when? And here we have again another central problem. The naming of the neighbor, the world—Who are you? Who is my neighbor? God cannot save (the first age's solution), man cannot save himself (the second age knew this but thought it was an argument for the truth of the first age), for only communities can heal. The concern of the new age is the shaping of healing communities, just as at the close of the second age, we were given a superbly fashioned therapy (psychoanalysis) to save us from our sick communities: family, nation, church. The characteristics, models, heroes of this age are harder to see, for we are just beginning to feel what it is like to live partly in it: Marshall McLuhan; style as our desire, rather than goal or value; cool; the Beatles; the New Left; "what's happening";

transcending the self-world distinction; post-historical, beyond Jesus, post-Christian.

Now everybody knows that historical periods, if they exist at all, never fit neatly together. There are always overlapping edges. The problem of the self is radically posed deep within the first age in Augustine's *Confessions,* and decisively at the close of the age in lay mysticism and nominalism. It can, therefore, be suggested that mysticism is the religion event that gets its genuine power by standing at the juncture of the first and the second age, the buffer between both, drawing from both, a help and a threat to both.

The problem of the world is, of course, raised profoundly in the second age, fundamentally we can say by the 18th-century political revolutions. In this sense, the French Revolution is the true start of the third age, and the third age contains thus the idea of the death of God, and Karl Marx as chief interpreter.

4. *Community in the Strange New World*

Our religious revolution today is defined, I believe, by the fact that we stand at the intersection between what I have called the second and the third age. And I suspect that radical theology is an attempt to maintain that compromise position, with one foot in both eras, whatever that means.

The special problem of the third age, and thus the special problem for the radical theology, is community. Can the institutions of the second age, the so-called modern world, serve in the new age? What about family, school, university, church, nation? In the movement into the strange new world, do these old communities bear their own healing power, or can traditional revolutionary techniques be devised to change them. Or must we look for another?

At the end of the second age, we asked about our identity, and at the start of the third age, we raised the question of politics: community and power. What are the communities that can heal us, and unto what end will the healing be done?

This is my half-serious proposal that may enable us to understand our religious situation. All of the mad ferment in our time, featured but not created by the media, the Christian atheists, the new Dionysians, the hip priests, the swinging nuns, and the religionless Christians—all these are heralds of the new age, living in the intersection, perplexed but not unto despair. Into this intersection, radical theology, among other things, is trying to move—to interpret, to understand and to help.

The radical theology is based, in one way or another, on the experience of the death of God, though it is increasingly clear that there are many ways of reading this experience, many ways of explaining it, and that all attempts to read and to explain are bound to fail. It was perhaps a terrible thing that "the death of God" should become a journalist event, but this was almost inevitable, and we should not complain. But perhaps one should spend some time in silence before this event, if event it is, and more time sitting before the poetic texts out of which the modern idea of the death of God springs: Blake, Jean-Paul, Heine, Emerson, Melville, Nietzsche, Arnold, Ibsen, Wallace Stevens, to name a few. Indeed, concentration on these texts may remind us that "death of God" makes sense only when we stay close to the poetic context out of which the idea comes, and that it doesn't make much sense when we try to depoetize, demythologize it, and put it into ordinary categories of historical space and time. As "event", in a literal historical sense, "death of God" is neither serviceable nor intelligible. As metaphor it is elusive but helpful, and bears a meaning that "absence", "eclipse", "disappearance" do not. In the idea of language-event, something that has happened to our speaking, we may have the best way of speaking about the death of God.

But we must learn to trust many different ways of describing what has happened to us religiously, and if "death of God" does not work for some, it should not be insisted on. But the real burden of radical theology is not a theory of the divine disappearance, but an interpretation of Christianity without God.

Death of God is, after all, a myth, and we need as few of these as possible. The point is: What are your expectations, how do you do your work? Does the Christian God function as a present reality or not? If not, then there is a doing without, and this entails both theological and practical tasks of considerable complexity and difficulty.

5. *New Work and New Thought*

The radical theologies, then, share this recognition that a new thing has taken place and that new work and new thought are required. Why has it happened? What is it that has made it possible, even necessary, for Christians to live without God? Here we find a rather large variety of answers. For some, science or philosophy have produced certain epistemological challenges that talk about God cannot meet. For others, death of God is a mythic-historic event related to the self-emptying of Jesus on the cross, and is thus to be described as part of the divine intention rather than as an outer event in the lives of men. For still others, the modern experiences of innocent suffering are unlike all others, and as such they have rendered much of the conventional God talk suspect, so that nothing like the traditional words can dare be uttered.

For me, the contemporary experience of the death of God is primarily related to a change, fully understood only in our time, in the relation between man and the world. Now this is so vague as to be hardly intelligible, and it needs to be carefully explained. Why, we may ask, has our current religious crisis taken this form? Why has the experience of the death of God emerged just now? Why didn't it come at the time of the scientific revolution of the 17th century? At the time of the political revolutions of the 18th century? In response to the industrial revolution? Why just today? Because, I suspect, of what we are coming to understand as the technological revolution of our time, and particularly because of the impact of technology on our sensibilities, our language, our feelings. Modern technology is taking on the whole world, the whole dedivinized cosmos, and, as the moralists often say, installing man as lord of things. It is improving on creation, making alterations in our world and in our bodies (one has only to think of the pharmacological revolution and the new attitudes to the body this already entails—both psychedelic and birth-control drugs come to mind). It is this that has annihilated our sense of piety and awe and thus our capacity to speak to or about God. There is still a world we do not know, but we are not afraid of it. There is still mystery and ignorance and wonder and awe. But we cannot mythologize it, we cannot trust these experiences of "not knowing" as being able to point to the meaning of God. This new relation to the world, it seems to me, is the central fact of our time, and it is the decisive spiritual event that enables us more clearly to understand the experience of the death of God.

Man, therefore, can move into his world, into his future, with a new measured calmness. He need not fear its mystery, its demons, its depth. Wallace Stevens has called this new situation "walking barefoot into reality". And it appears to have two elements. It is partly a passive thing, plunging into the world, abandoning your will to power over it, letting it show you its splendor and power. It is also a very active relation, hopeful, confident, calm. There are, of course, real evils, and death is one of them. But they can either be overcome, these evils, by new forms of therapy or new kinds of politics or new communities of love or action, or they can be coped with.

The spirituality of radical theology is politics, its aim is the calling of communities. Its prayer is intercession, and its key biblical text, its Romans 1:17, so to speak—is Mark 9:37.

The real intellectual work of radical theology lies before it. Its agenda includes the clarification of the idea of the death of God in the 19th century, the development of a Christology along the lines of the traditional *imitatio* theme, the idea of the birth, the death and resurrection of God as language event. But this will be done slowly, in monographic bits and pieces. This theology is now genuinely cutting across traditional boundaries, and both Jewish and Catholic responses are taking form. With the journalistic phase at an end, with the offense all given and received, it can now take its modest role as an intellectual and political-ethical experiment, whose failure or success is still a matter for determination. For living and thinking as a Christian without God is, to say the least, an odd and difficult aim.

PART II
BIBLIOGRAPHICAL
SURVEY

John Edward Crouzet, O.S.B./*North Bath, England*

A DISCUSSION:
The Bishop of Woolwich's Book
The New Reformation

Although the Bishop of Woolwich has a considerable reputation as a Scripture scholar, *The New Reformation,*[1] like its predecessor, *Honest to God,*[2] was addressed to a far wider public than would have read any of his academic works. Robinson, indeed, complains that the state of academic theology is such that if an academic theologian feels the need to examine live questions which are of practical concern in the world today, he is forced to do it as a sideline. Yet it has been just such amateur works as Robinson's *On Being the Church in the World* [3] and *Honest to God,* which have, as he says, created the ferment. Robinson complains that these books are not "what would be regarded, professionally speaking, as serious theology, of the sort that I would dare include in a submission, say, for a Doctorate of Divinity—though I reckon they probably include as much original theology as any of my academically respectable books".[4]

It is possible that if *Honest to God* had been submitted to the rigors of academic discipline, it would never have appeared. And that, in view of the interest it aroused among people not normally concerned with theological questions, would have been

[1] London, 1965.
[2] London, 1963.
[3] London, 1960.
[4] *The New Reformation,* pp. 67-8.

a pity. However, if *Honest to God* was unsatisfactory in that it revealed a misunderstanding of many of the "traditional" views the author was anxious to rebut,[5] *The New Reformation* is more successful because less speculative in its scope. It reflects in a more practical way the questioning and ideas of a bishop who is committed by his office to an attempt to marry the traditional structures of the Church of England to the needs of life in a modern city.

In writing this book, it was the Bishop's conviction that the signs of ferment stirring within the Churches are so all-embracing as to justify the analogy with the 16th-century Reformation, and he is concerned to "explore what a new Reformation might mean".[6] One thing that it does not mean, at least in its beginnings, is the elaboration of new theological and ecclesiastical systems. "In the long run those who change history most are not those who supply a new set of answers but those who allow a new set of questions. And it was indeed this latter possibility, rather than the theological and ecclesiastical systems in which their work took shape, that represented the real achievement of the Reformers."[7] Reform is in the first place a liberation of the power which is pent up beneath the oppressiveness of established forms and structures. When these are questioned and, where necessary, broken down (though Robinson turns out later in the book to be cautious about this) the power is released, and the removal of an accumulation of bric-a-brac allows the "Easter light" to "shine all the whiter". In this, too, there is a parallel with the 16th century: " 'I am quite sure,' wrote the young Luther, 'that the Church will never be reformed unless we get rid of canon law, scholastic theology, philosophy and logic as they are studied today, and put something else in their place.' If pressed about WHAT he would put in their place, I suspect he would have been less sure. I have every sympathy with him.

---

[5] See *The Honest to God Debate*, ed. J. Robinson and D. Edwards (London, 1963), and, in particular, the review by H. McCabe; also E. Mascall, *The Secularisation of Christianity* (London, 1965), pp. 106-89.

[6] *The New Reformation*, p. 16.

[7] *Ibid.*, p. 12.

In fact, however, what shone through was NOT what he put in their place (his successors filled the gap with an equally deadly Protestant scholasticism) but what he left exposed." [8]

Robinson is obsessed with the image of the Church as "an archaic and well-protected institution for the preservation of something which is irrelevant and incredible",[9] and this is in spite of the fact that something comparable to our *aggiornamento* has been going on in the Church of England for several decades. The inadequacy of structural streamlining, as well of the biblical, ecumenical and liturgical movements, is that they leave relatively untouched the overall question of the truth of Christianity, of the credible revelation of God to the 20th century and tend to exclude the "awkward questions and needs of the irreligious moderns".[10] The first requisite, then, of a new Reformation, is a process of "stripping down", of the Church "going through its baggage to discover how much it can better do without, both in doctrine and organization".[11]

I

FAITH AND DOCTRINE

Robinson approaches the problem by describing the vehement reaction of a group of Christians and non-Christians, whom he invited to a weekend conference in 1964, against the Church's traditional credal and liturgical formularies. "One of the group had said to me on first meeting: 'All the Church seems to have to say to me is: Come to Evensong and stand up and say the Creed, and this I feel I neither want to nor can.' " [12] Any Catholic who has been through a traditional seminary course of theology will know what the Bishop means when he says: "I suspect it reflects a deep-seated resistance to any attempt to start from given truths, to prescribe the definition in advance of the

8 *Ibid.*, p. 19.
9 *Ibid.*, p. 20.
10 *The Honest to God Debate*, p. 20.
11 *The New Reformation*, p. 20.
12 *Ibid.*, p. 40.

experience." [13] The irrelevance of the academic training of the clergy to their subsequent involvement in the world is no doubt related to this: "The traditional theology purveyed by the universities is essentially prolegomena. It is the grammar of the subject and is linguistically and historically centered. However much it may be made relevant by imaginative teaching, the center of gravity (which I suppose is somewhere between the first century and the fifth) is miles away from the center of concern. The result, as one sees from the clergy, is that most of us who read theology as students quickly give it up as a matter of living concern." [14]

It is true that the Anglican theological training normally comprises a predominant proportion of positive studies, whereas the Catholic tends to be predominantly speculative. But perhaps the time has come when we should ask whether the teaching of theology as a total, deductive system on the medieval pattern is adequate to the needs of modern Christians. It will always be the task of theology to systematize, to work out the relationship between cause and effect and to present its results in that order, but in the order of cognition in the individual any system is bound at some stage to appear as a straitjacket, as a prescription rather than as an analysis of his experience.

Although the Bishop of Woolwich speaks somewhat sensationally ("the whole theological front is now wide open: the very foundations are now exposed"), *The New Reformation* shows signs of more caution than did *Honest to God*. In the matter of doctrine, as of Church organization, he sees it as necessary to reform from both ends, that is, by starting both from within the tradition (what he calls the "experimental" approach) and from the secular end (the "exploratory" approach). It is with the latter that he is concerned in this book.

Following Horst Symanowski,[15] he maintains that whereas the first Reformation began from the question, "How can I find a

[13] *Loc. cit.*
[14] *Ibid.*, p. 68.
[15] *Gegen die Weltfremdheit* (Munich, 1960), p. 19.

gracious God?" and gave the reply, "by faith alone", which issued in the doctrine of election, of the Church as the company of the elect, "a congregation of faithful men, in which the pure Word of God is preached, and the sacraments duly administered",[16] this question and reply evoke no response in men of today: "For the fact remains that to larger and larger numbers of our generation this is simply not gospel, it evokes no sense of good news . . . For the world is not asking 'How can I find a gracious God?' It is asking 'How can I find a gracious neighbor?' And it is starting, not from the 'elect people of God', but from what the most representative collection of photographs of our time called 'the family of man'. It begins, not from revelation, in which it has no prior confidence, but from relationships, which it is prepared to treat with a greater seriousness than any generation before it." [17] Robinson admits that there are other questions that people are asking, and he mentions Teilhard de Chardin as one who starts from nature rather than from history, but it must be agreed that he has stated, in somewhat quaint language, the concern which is most immediate for the majority of modern Westerners.

The approach which the Bishop would then advocate is of a theology that starts from Christ as the way into the Father. He considers that if any text proves central to the new Reformation, as "sola fide" did to the old, it will be "He who has seen me has seen the Father." [18] And he goes on to elaborate his idea of the encounter with the Son of Man incognito by appealing to the "parable" of the Sheep and Goats. "If men are to see Christ, and therefore God, they can only do it through the one who comes to them, in the first instance, not as a messianic figure, but as one of themselves, as Fred or Harry or the man across the street." [19] Together with the "parable" of the Sheep and Goats, Robinson places the story of the disciples on the road to Emmaus, the final appearance of Jesus by the lakeside in John

[16] *39 Articles*, Art. XIX.
[17] *The New Reformation*, pp. 33-4.
[18] Jn. 14, 9.
[19] *The New Reformation*, p. 35.

21, and the washing of his disciples' feet in John 13 as instances where Christ discloses himself by appearing first under the guise of the "gracious neighbor". Indeed Robinson places so much stress on this idea that he speaks of it as being "of normative importance for our generation" [20] and as having "a distinctive significance for our age".[21]

The Bishop is almost certainly right, again, in seeing this as the area in which theological concern is most likely to be centered fruitfully: "Perhaps the primary task of theology and of the Church in our generation could be described as making such a meeting possible again. For the effect of the Church's work has been to strip the Christ of his incognito. It has placarded him to men as the Son of God without allowing them to meet him as the Son of Man. It has said to men: 'We have the Christ, defined in our creeds, present in our churches, speaking with final authority in our codes. Come to him there. Acknowledge him as Lord and God.' It has been a deductive rather than an inductive approach, presenting them from the start with the answers they must accept if they are to believe." [22]

The prescription of experience without allowing it to ask its own questions may have much to do with the inability of people to accept Christ as presented by the Church. And the Bishop is surely right when he says that people should be allowed to "work the sum out for themselves". But there are difficulties in this approach. They center round the notion of "inductive". Robinson uses this word in two related contexts: first to signify an approach that would start from human experience, from the questions which men are asking themselves today, from the area of their greatest concern, personal relationships: "To ask men to believe in the doctrine or to accept the revelation before they see it for themselves as the definition of their experience and the depth of their relationship, is to ask what to this generation, with its schooling in an empirical approach to everything,

20 *Ibid.*
21 *Ibid.,* p. 36.
22 *Ibid.,* p. 37.

seems increasingly hollow." [23] Secondly the word is used to describe a presentation of Christ which does not begin from the Chalcedonian definitions or even from any of the titles applied to him by the early Church, but which "starts from the other end" by considering him as a human being. "It [the inductive approach to Christian doctrine] does insist that the ends are only to be reached from the beginning—and the beginning for men today, as for the first disciples, is from Jesus as a completely human man—whatever more they may be compelled to see in him." [24] He illustrates this "way in" by taking as examples the traditional doctrines of the Virgin birth and the pre-existence of Christ, doctrines which only came to be articulated after his disciples had encountered Christ as a man.

No one, I think, will dispute that if by "inductive" the Bishop means simply starting from the end which is nearest to our own experience, in either of the above senses, he is making a valuable observation on the inadequacy (an understatement) of our way of thinking about and presenting our faith. But, although there is no question of pressing the strict scientific meaning of the word "inductive"—the Bishop is clearly using it in a loose sense—it must mean something more than that. Indeed, the idea of starting from the other end, from experience, would be of little value to him if it didn't. For Robinson it means "discovering the revelation in the relationship"; it is the act by which "the revelation discloses itself as the depth and meaning of the relationship". He is on his guard in this section of the book against being attacked for turning his back on a theology of revelation and replacing it with a "natural" theology "which begins with the presuppositions of human nature and hopes to arrive at Christianity from them".[25] The difficulty arises, however, not with regard to the supernaturality of the act of faith (though the Bishop might be reluctant to use that term), or the gratuitous quality of the revelation, but with the idea of an "inductive"

[23] *Ibid.*, p. 40.
[24] *Ibid.*, p. 42.
[25] *Ibid.*, p. 34.

progression from the neighbor in the "parable" of the Sheep and
Goats to the revelation of Christ; that men will be able to see
Christ, and therefore God, "through the one who comes to
them, in the first instance, not as a messianic figure, but as one
of themselves, as Fred or Harry or the man across the street".
The weakness of this "way in" is that the agnostic can still ask
why it is necessary to believe that it is Christ that he is meeting,
that Christ is present now in power. The "Man for others" may
well be the model or "definition of a genuinely human existence",[26] but this is not a sufficient basis for an act of faith. What
is lacking is any idea of an ontological link between the "gracious neighbor" and the risen Christ. This does not invalidate
Bishop Robinson's thesis that personal relations are the area in
which to start asking the questions. Indeed, he seems aware of
this difficulty when he says: "Perhaps the primary task of theology and of the Church in our generation could be described
as making such a meeting [i.e., as in the Emmaus story] possible
again." [27] We can only agree with him.

However, the Bishop of Woolwich does appear to undermine
the possibility of any such theology being elaborated, in an
earlier section of the book, where he outlines his idea of the
"pure theology" which is to characterize the new Reformation.
He quotes with approval van Buren[28] as "accurately describing
the difference between us and our ancestors" when he writes:
"We are saying that it is possible today to be agnostic about
'other-worldly' powers and beings, but that people matter, that
we live in a world in which 'I' is not 'you' and neither is completely assimilable to 'it' or even to 'he'. We are urging that
Buber's distinction matters more than distinctions between eter-
nity and time, infinity and finite, and many other distinctions
that mattered to Christians in another age." And again: "In almost every field of human learning, the metaphysical and cosmo-
logical aspect has disappeared and the subject matter has been

[26] *Ibid.*, p. 42.
[27] *Ibid.*, p. 37.
[28] *The Secular Meaning of the Gospel* (New York, 1963), p. 195.

'limited' to the human, the historical, the empirical. Theology cannot escape this tendency if it is to be a serious mode of contemporary thought."

One can see why the Bishop quotes these passages; it is in reaction to a theology which claimed to provide a complete spiritual map of the universe so that, as he puts it, medieval theology could discourse with confidence on limbo and purgatory, and Reformation theology dismiss them with equal confidence. The theological map can now no longer be so exhaustive, and is necessarily full of gaps at the edges. Vatican Council II speaks of an "order or hierarchy of truths", which are ranged according as "they vary in their relationship to the foundation of the Christian faith",[29] and it is not far from this to the statement of Bonhoeffer, quoted by Robinson, that "on the borders it seems to me better to hold our peace".[30]

But there is an ambiguity inherent in Robinson's theological "agnosticism" which appears in his statement that "as soon as we pass beyond the limited area verifiable in the experience of our relationships with other people and with things, there is nothing to count for or against the truth of our assertions".[31] If taken in the context of the two quotations from van Buren above, this could mean that nothing which cannot be experienced empirically in the same way as we experience our relationships with persons and things can enter into theology, and all possibility of transcendence would be denied. If, on the other hand, it is taken to mean that this must be the point on which theological concern is centered and to which it constantly returns, then he is making a statement about theological relevance which requires attention.

[29] *Decree on Ecumenism*, n. 11.
[30] *The New Reformation*, p. 23.
[31] *Loc. cit.*

II

CHURCH STRUCTURES

With regard to ecclesiastical structures and organization, Robinson offers a program of "stripping down" and "travelling light" parallel to his reformation in faith and doctrine. He starts from the same fearful image of the contemporary Church as "an archaic and well protected institution for the preservation of something that is irrelevant and incredible", and from a certain uneasiness that all the updating and *aggiornamento* which he acknowledges to have taken place in the Church (of England) during recent decades may, in fact, represent a deeper entrenchment.

The Bishop's principal criticism of existing Church structures is that they are parallel to and separate from those of secular society. The Church has a heavy investment in plant which, if anything, cuts it off from the world. "The basic trouble is not that the Church has been too affluent—it is chronically short of money—but that it has used it on building its own structures (literally or metaphorically) rather than on serving in those of others. It has been an institution alongside, not the leaven within, the world it exists to change." [32] In stating this view, Robinson is echoing what is being said by a number of contemporary Christian thinkers,[33] but if his idea is not original, it is forcefully presented.

The most characteristic example of ecclesiastical plant to come under Robinson's criticism is the residential parish congregation, to which, he tells us, well over 90 percent of the clergy of the Church of England are committed. In accordance with his principles of reform from both ends, he does not want, or even think possible, the simple abolition of the parish congregation. But he questions whether this type of church can any longer be considered as the normal model for community wor-

[32] *Ibid.*, p. 27.
[33] Cf. Harvey Cox, *The Secular City* (New York, 1965). For the application of this idea to a particular context, see *Theology and the University*, ed. J. Coulson (London, 1964).

ship. "We can all think of dozens of people who, if they wanted to identify themselves with some Christian concern or do something worthwhile with their lives, would regard joining a local congregation or working through it as about the least relevant step to take. And this is not necessarily because their commitment to Christ is in doubt (it applies to many ordinands and clergy), but because the congregation appears to be a structure so unrelated to the real centers of men's lives and to the places where decisions are taken." [34]

Reformation must come, the Bishop tells us, quoting the words of another writer,[35] by the Church "allowing the forms of her renewed life to grow around the shapes of worldly need". "The whole tendency of the Reformation-Counter-Reformation era was to think of the Church in terms of the gathered or excommunicating group. It defined the Church when it was out of the world, as the salt piled, clean and white in the cellar, as the leaven unmixed with the meal. And this is precisely when it is not being itself or performing its essential function. For it is distinctively itself when it cannot be seen or tasted for itself at all, but when it is transforming whatever it is in." [36] As the first Reformation brought about the "dissolution" of the monasteries, so it will be characteristic of the new Reformation that the salt should normally be "at least 95 percent of the time in 'solution'. The role of the Church is that of servant. As such it is not proper for it to construct its own "imperium": "The house of God is not the Church, but the world. The Church is the servant, and the first characteristic of a servant is that he lives in someone else's house, not his own. Paradoxically the Church is also the son, the one who has the freedom of the house. But Christians only too often have celebrated this freedom as soon as they have had the chance, by setting up on their own." [37] The Church is to be an "open society", an "accepting community",

[34] *The New Reformation*, p. 90.
[35] C. Williams, *Where in the World?* (New York, 1963), p. 59.
[36] *The New Reformation*, p. 47.
[37] *Ibid.*, p. 92.

the characteristic of which is that it is "prepared to meet men where they are and to accept them for what they are".[38]

The Bishop works out the lines along which this idea of the Church would be realized in practice, in the abolition of what he calls "the clergy line" according to which the clergy form a kind of upper stratum in the Church and the laity are envisaged as their "helpers"; in the abolition of an exclusively professional and, therefore, to some extent segregated priesthood; in the abolition of the "sex line" which prevents women from playing a responsible role in the Church; in a reversal of roles whereby the ministry of the Church is seen primarily as the work of the laity, with the clergy as specialist helpers; with consequently a renewed theology undertaken by lay Christians reflecting upon the meaning "in Christ" of the history which they, as secular men, have the responsibility of shaping; and a renewed liturgy which has its roots in the ordinary life of society.

The Bishop makes no claim to originality for these ideas: his book is a patchwork of quotations from contemporary writers. But the general direction he gives to these ideas is impressive and deserves careful reflection. They suffer, however, from a lack of clarity in the underlying ecclesiological premise. In conclusion, I would like to draw attention to this.

Robinson uses the distinction of Tillich between the "latent" and the "manifest" Church. The latter is, in the Bishop's words, "the dedicated nucleus of those who actively acknowledge Jesus as Lord and have committed themselves to membership and mission within the visible, sacramental fellowship of the Spirit". [39] The former is, in Tillich's words, quoted by Robinson, "an indefinite historical group which, within paganism, Judaism or humanism, actualizes the New Being".[40] And Robinson adds: "It corresponds with the distinction I referred to earlier between the Christ acknowledged and the Christ incognito. And 'where Christ is'—where either Christ is—'there is the Church'. In its

[38] *Ibid.*, p. 46.
[39] *Ibid.*, p. 48.
[40] *The Theology of Paul Tillich*, ed. C. Kegley and R. Bretall (New York, 1952), p. 259.

latent form of existence it may not be organized, it may not be able to say 'Lord, Lord', and within it the pure Word of God is certainly not preached nor the sacraments duly administered. And yet it may be nearer the truth to view it as the latent Church than as the godless world." [41] With this we can only agree. But Robinson is on his guard against churchmen who will accuse him of reducing the Gospel to "mere humanism" and of "giving in to secularism"; yet he opens himself to precisely this charge because of the blurring of his thought at this point. For it is his thesis that the Church must "respect rather than remove the incognitos under which the parable of the Sheep and Goats alone shows it possible for the Christ to meet and judge the mass of men". This is an ambiguous statement which is not clarified by the appeal he makes, first to the Bible and then to the analogy with the Communist Party of Soviet Russia. The first purports to question the fact that "it is taken for granted, both inside and outside the Church, that the eventual, if not the immediate, aim of all it does is to elicit that commitment", (i.e., to becoming members of the manifest Church),[42] but what he in effect shows from the Book of Revelation is, not that this should not be the Church's aim, but that it will fail to achieve this aim, "at any rate within this age".

In the analogy with the Russian Communist Party, the Party corresponds to the manifest Church, and the universal socialist society it seeks to promote corresponds to the kingdom of God. The tactics of the Party, he tells us, are not based on the assumption that all Russians will become Communists, in the sense of acknowledging a conscious ideological commitment and discipline. Obviously the "tactics" of the manifest Church are not based on the assumption that all men will become professed Christians. But this does not preclude the Church from having this as its aim. What the Bishop is anxious to affirm is that the Church should show "an utterly disinterested concern for persons for their own sake", and not treat them as potential ma-

41 *The New Reformation*, pp. 47-8.
42 *Loc. cit.*

terial for boosting its own authority as an institution. But if the active proselytizing attitude is to be deplored, there is still the possibility of expansion through the un-self-conscious concern that the Bishop seems to be advocating. We must agree with him that respect for persons is of supreme importance, but this respect could be lacking if it were accepted as a principle that they are better left as part of the latent Church. It is on this point that Robinson, no doubt from a justifiable fear of the individual's autonomy being violated, leaves us uncertain.

Lest these criticisms should appear to belittle the value of Robinson's book and the urgency of the challenge it makes to traditional Christianity, I shall end by quoting the question he puts at the head of his outline of the forms the new Reformation should take: "Do we affirm the Easter faith in our time by insisting that God raised Jesus from the dead or by daring to risk ourselves in the confidence that God will raise us from the dead? Can we do the former without the latter?" [43]

[43] From C. Ebb Mundun in *MOTIVE* (January, 1963).

Stanislaw Napiórkowski, O.F.M. Conv./*Lublin, Poland*

The Present Position in Mariology

The problem of Mary is not mentioned explicitly in the formula for the admission of new converts (to the Lutheran Church) from the Catholic Church.[1] This does not mean that mariology does not form an obstacle in the ecumenical dialogue. However, awareness of the organic link existing between the fundamental premises of both Catholic and Protestant mariology will enable us in this article to determine how far an ecumenical dialogue is possible in the field of mariology. As for Chapter VIII of *Lumen Gentium,* this article will allow us to take stock of what can be expected from conciliar mariology.

Yet, not all mariology flows directly from the basic theological propositions. Like other aspects of the two theologies, it has matured down the centuries and bears the visible marks of multiple conditioning—historical, geographical, psychological and so on. Mariology in Latin countries like Spain or Italy differs perceptibly from that of Germanic countries such as Holland or Germany. The stamp which Scholasticism gave it is different from the one bestowed by the New Theology. On the Protestant side, the mariology of Taizé[2] is not the same as that

[1] "Aufnahme von Konvertiten aus der römischen Kirche," in *Agende für die Evangelische Landeskirche* (Berlin, 1895) 38.
[2] Cf. M. Thurian, "Marie dans la Bible et dans l'Église," in *Dialogue*

113

professed at the University of Heidelburg;[3] nor is the pietist movement's attitude to Mary identical with the one which liberal Protestantism was to adopt. All this testifies to the extreme elasticity of the doctrinal positions of the two denominations and justifies our treating the subject from the new ecumenical points of view now opening up in mariology.

Max Thurian of Taizé, one of the most ecumenically-minded of Protestant theologians, expresses the hope that so far as the sacraments, grace and even the Church are concerned a reconciliation can be expected; but it does not seem to him that as much can be said of the problem of mariology and Marian devotion.[4]

Another Protestant theologian just as sincerely wedded to the idea of ecumenism, H. Asmussen of the Lutheran Church, reckons that there is apparently no question on which the various Christian denominations are so deeply divided as that of the place of Mary in the economy of salvation.[5] Protestants, wrote Professor R. Mehl in 1957, regard Catholic mariology as a sort of fatal labyrinth which spells death to evangelical faith and in which all the heresies of Catholicism are concentrated; that is why to him the total rejection of the whole of Catholic mariology is an indispensable means of setting the Protestant conscience at rest.[6] W. von Loewenich sees mariology as the prin-

---

sur la Vierge (Paris-Lyon, 1950) 107-139; idem, "Mariology Reformed," in Ways of Worship: The Report of a Theological Commission of Faith and Order (London, 1951) 289-323; idem, "Le dogme de l'Assomption," in Verbum Caro 5 (1951), 2-50; idem, "Evolution du catholicisme. Mariologie," in Verbum Caro 10 (1956) 90-92; idem, "Le mémorial des saints. Essai de compréhension évangélique d'un aspect de la piété catholique," in Verbum Caro 13 (1959) 7-28; idem, Marie, Mère du Seigneur, Figure de l'Église (Taizé, ²1962); P. Y. Emery, "L'unité des croyants au ciel et sur la terre" (Taizé, 1962).

[3] Evangelisches Gutachten zur Dogmatisierung der leiblichen Himmelfahrt Mariens (Munich, 1950).

[4] Mariology Reformed, 289.

[5] H. Asmussen, Maria, die Mutter Gottes (Stuttgart, ³1960) 39.

[6] R. Mehl, Du catholicisme romain, Approche et interprétation (Paris-Neuchâtel, 1957) 91.

cipal point of conflict,[7] while in the view of W. Künneth the two conceptions, Catholic and Protestant, of the Virgin Mary are two radically different worlds with a deep chasm between them; he sees no possibility of erecting a bridge across this gulf.[8] This position is shared by other Protestant theologians such as F. Heiler,[9] P. Maury,[10] W. Meyer,[11] K. Nitzschke[12] and P. Bourget.[13] Catholic theologians conversant with the problems of ecumenism hold similar opinions. J. Sartory, for example, says that mariology and Marian devotion constitute the principal point of conflict between the Catholic Church and the Protestant Churches.[14] R. Laurentin compares the mariological problem with that of the papacy so far as difficulties for the ecumenical movement are concerned.[15]

Such are the terms in which theologians presented the mariological problem before Vatican Council II. Our aim here is to examine carefully how and to what extent conciliar mariology allows us to span this gulf, so recently described as unbridgeable. The remarks which follow are grouped around four questions: concepts of mariology, the theological methods applied in mariology, the problem of the mediation of Mary and, finally, that of the cult of the divine Mother.

[7] W. von Loewenich, *Der moderne Katholizismus. Erscheinung und Probleme* (Witten, 1955) 275.

[8] W. Künneth, *Christus oder Maria? Ein evangelisches Wort zum Mariendogma* (Berlin-Spandau, 1950) 28.

[9] F. Heiler, compte-rendu de P. Sträter Katholische Marienkunde, in *Eine Heilige Kirche* 1 (1955-56) 87.

[10] P. Maury, "La Vierge Marie dans le catholicisme contemporain," in *Le protestantisme et la Vierge Marie* (Paris, 1950) 26-27.

[11] W. Meyer, "Maria als Bild der Gnade und Heiligkeit," in *Begegnung der Christen. Studien evangelischer und katholischer Theologen* (Stuttgart-Frankfurt am Main, ²1960) 586.

[12] K. Nitzschke, "Maria, Marienverehrung," in *Evangelisches Kirchenlexikon* (Göttingen, 1958), 1245.

[13] P. Bourguet, *Le protestantisme et la Vierge Marie*, 10-11.

[14] T. Sartory, "Maria und die getrennten Brüder," in *Gloria Dei* 5 (1954) 224.

[15] R. Laurentin, *La question mariale* (Paris, 1963); trans.: *Mary's Place in the Church* (London and New York, 1965) 134.

I

CONCEPTS OF MARIOLOGY

Two expressions have found their way into Catholic mariology during the last few years: christotypical mariology and ecclesiotypical mariology.[16] These two types are not easy to describe. The essential difference between them lies in the manner in which Mary's role in the work of redemption is conceived. Christotypical mariologians lay a great deal of emphasis on the analogy between the function of Mary and the redemptive function of Christ. They declare repeatedly and emphatically that Mary's role, thus understood, does not diminish in the slightest the perfection of the work accomplished by Christ, the one and only mediator; but they maintain nonetheless that Mary's cooperation in the objective fact of redemption can in no way be regarded as an *appendix accidentalis*.[17] Their statements imply that Mary stands by the side of Christ, facing humanity with him, rather than by the side of humanity and facing him. Mariologians of an ecclesiotypical cast of mind, which has become more topical again after the publication of the studies by O. Semmelroth,[18] H. Köster[19] and A. Müller[20] on the theme of Mary and the Church, tend rather to put the emphasis on Mary's in-

[16] The expression "ecclesiotypical mariology" is less felicitous than "christotypical mariology". It is apposite only insofar as the functions of Mary are considered on the pattern of the functions of the Church; it is inaccurate, for we do not speak of the Church as the type of Mary, but inversely: Mary is the type of the Church. The expressions "christotypical aspect" and "ecclesiotypical aspect" were suggested by H. M. Köster at the International Mariological and Mariàl Congress held at Lourdes. Cf. *Maria et Ecclesia* II (Rome, 1959) 21-51.

[17] C. Dillenschneider, *Marie au service de notre rédemption* (Haguenau, 1947) 369.

[18] The formula "Maria-Urbild der Kirche" is regarded by O. Semmelroth as the most accurate expression of the mariological principle.

[19] H. Köster, *Die Magd des Herrn. Theologische Versuche und Uberlegungen* (Limbourg, ²1954); *idem, Unus Mediator. Gedanken zur marianischen Frage* (Limbourg, 1950).

[20] A. Müller, *Ecclesia-Maria* (Fribourg, 1955). Cf. *idem*, "Um die Grundlagen der Mariologie," in *Divus Thomas* 29 (1951) 386-401; *idem*, "Fragen und Aussichten der heutigen Mariologie," in *Fragen der Theologie heute* (Einsiedeln, 1957) 301-317.

destructible bonds with humanity. They remind us that the objective work of redemption is the exclusive affair of the one and only mediator; they draw attention to the fact that the Gospel speaks not only of the union between the Virgin and Christ but also of a clear separation between Mother and Son in what concerns Christ's accomplishment of the work of salvation. This ecclesiotypical tendency has its own vocabulary; it talks of Mary as the type of the Church, the most perfect member of the Church, the model of humility, faith, charity, devotion to God, obedience and docility, and of Mary the servant of the Lord.[21] In this conception Mary stands clearly by the side of humanity, facing with it their common redeemer.

It is easy to see that it is not unimportant for the ecumenical dialogue which of these two conceptions wins the day in Catholic theology. Even those of the Protestant theologians who are most favorable to Catholicism confront it with this serious question:

"Is Mary on the side of God or on the side of men?" (writes Asmussen) "This question in particular requires a clear answer because at the present moment there is hardly any point of doctrine on which the different denominations are so sharply divided as on this one. Evangelical Christians feel that in the Catholic devotion to Mary the boundary between God and man is being eroded. In the last analysis the decisive factor is not what our Catholic brethren really mean. They would first have to admit that they are understood to imply that in the Mother of God there appears by the side of Christ a further mediator of salvation; and it is not quite clear whether this second mediator stands on God's side against us or on our side against God." [22]

---

[21] Just as many cardinals and bishops suggested deleting from the conciliar text the title "Mediatrix" because it does not occur in the Bible, so on the other side many voices were raised in favor of the removal of the term "ancilla Domini", which is nevertheless evangelical. Cf. R. Le Déaut, "Marie et L'Ecriture dans le chapitre VIII," in *Etudes Mariales* 22 (1965) 59.

[22] H. Asmussen, *op. cit.*, 39.

Protestant theology is gradually beginning to abandon its claim to be entirely unaware of the problems raised by the Marian question.[23] It has already given us several attempts at the construction of a Protestant mariology. It is significant that the theme of Mary and the Church begins to appear in them. The vast study by Max Thurian[24] deserves a place in the front rank. Pastor J. de Saussure's beautiful Meditation[25] must also be mentioned. Protestant theologians gladly recognize that the Mother of our Lord constitutes for the Christian a gracious model of numerous virtues, particularly of humility, faith and the service of God. They call her, though rarely, figure of the Church,[26] type of the Church,[27] type of the believing Church,[28] exemplary witness of the Church,[29] true representative of the Church,[30] personification of the Church,[31] archetype of the faithful of the new covenant and archetype of the Church,[32] and, in short, the type of every believing Christian.[33]

[23] Particular attention is merited by W. Delius, *Geschichte der Marienverehrung*, (Munich-Bâle, 1963); F. W. Künneth, *Maria, das römisch-katholische Bild vom christlichen Menschen. Der Zusammenhang von Antropologie und Mariologie in der gegenwärtigen römisch-katholischen Theologie des deutschen Sprachraume* (Berlin, 1961); C. A. de Ridder, *Maria Medeverlosseres? De Discussie in de huidige Rooms Katholieke Theologie over de medewerking van de Moeder Gods in het verlossingswerk* (Kampen, 1961). A bibliography of the position of Protestant theology with regard to the dogma of the assumption of the Blessed Virgin Mary will be found in C. S. Napiórkowski, "Dogmat o wniebowzięciu Najświętszej Maryi Panny w świetle krytki protestanckiej, "Roczniki Tologiczno-Kanoniczne," in *Annales de Théologie et de Droit Canon* 13 (1966) 77-92.

[24] *Marie, Mère du Seigneur, Figure de l'Église* (Taizé, ²1962).

[25] J. de Saussure, "Méditation sur la Vierge, figure de l'Église," in *Dialogue sur la Vierge*, 81-106.

[26] H. Roux, "Pour une doctrine biblique de la Vierge," in *Le protestantisme et la Vierge Marie* (Paris, 1950) 85.

[27] W. Graf, *Ja und Nein. Ein Konfessionsgespräch* (Munich, 1950) 99.

[28] H. Roux, *op. cit.*, 88.

[29] *Ibid.*, 81.

[30] W. Stählin, "Maria, die Mutter des Herrn. Ihr biblisches Bild," in *Symbolon* (Stuttgart, 1958) 115.

[31] J. de Saussure, *op. cit.*, 102.

[32] H. Lamparter, *Die Mutter unseres Herrn. Ein evang. Marienbuchlein* (Berlin-Dahlem, 1950) 23.

[33] M. Thurian, *Le dogme de l'Assomption*, 28.

Ecclesiotypical mariology has a real chance of becoming the object of both Catholic and Protestant thinking.

What is the position adopted in this respect by Chapter VIII of *Lumen Gentium*? Clear traces of the two opposing tendencies in mariology can be found. In the first section christotypical mariology makes itself felt in the importance given to the close union between the Virgin Mary and the Savior Christ. Yet it is very much toned down; no attempt is made to define the nature of Mary's cooperation in the objective event of redemption, a point on which the christological tendency in mariology had reached its peak in the era preceding the Council. The relationship between the Virgin and the Savior is described with the help of biblical texts almost entirely devoid of any theological interpretation.

Later on, the ecclesiotypical tendency is given more emphasis than the christotypical one. The former had already found expression in the modification of the original title of the schema. The title finally adopted places Mary *in Mysterio Christi et Ecclesiae*. The general tenor of the document is that Mary is above all the most perfect member of the Church, a member who by her faith, charity, submission and perfect union with Christ constitutes the type of the Church. It is not unimportant for the cause of ecumenism that the conciliar fathers preferred not to give Mary the title of Mother of the Church although this idea can indeed be discovered in the chapter, and the first schema borrowed it from Leo XIII.[34]

II

THE THEOLOGICAL METHOD

A reading of Chapter VIII provokes interesting thoughts on the theological method employed in it. For a proper appreciation of its ecumenical scope it will be useful to recall the typical mode of thought of the Protestant theologian. This is well re-

[34] No. 1. Cf. Léon XIII, Enc. *Adiutricem populi*, in H. Marin, *Documentos Marianos* (Madrid, 1954) 303.

flected in the confession of faith of the Reformed Church of France, the confession known as the Confession of La Rochelle:

"This Word is the rule of all truth and contains everything necessary for the service of God and our salvation . . ." [35]

The *Formula Concordiae,* a Lutheran document, describes the Bible as the sole norm and rule by which all dogmas must be judged.[36]

Founded as it is on scripture, in an exclusive sense, Protestantism is obliged to reject a mariology largely based on the authority of the Church's magisterium. This rejection affects all Catholic theology but more particularly mariology, insofar as the latter leans heavily on the declarations of the magisterium. In the last few decades in particular, Marian theology has drawn liberally on the extraordinary abundance of pontifical documents, whose authority has been more and more strongly emphasized. Thus, biblical mariology was gradually giving way to a mariology which might be described as "papal" and was often based on pontifical statements of a pastoral or homiletic character. This is true in particular of those propositions which can only be given a biblical foundation with extreme difficulty, for example, the universal dispensation of graces and certain conceptions of Mary's coredemption.[37]

The authors of the first schema on the Mother of God followed the line of papal mariology. This is how they explain their procedure in the preamble:

"The Council considers it opportune to explain briefly the place which the Mother of God and the Mother of men oc-

---

[35] *La Confession de la Rochelle,* nn. 4 et 5: Ed. *La Revue Réformée* 3 (1952) 10; cf. *La Confession Helvétique Postérieure* (Neuchâtel-Paris, 1944) 44-46; *La Confession de la Foi des Églises Réformées Wallones et Flamandes des Pays-Bas, art. VII* (Paris, 1934) 185.

[36] "Credimus, confitemur et docemus unicam regulam et normam, secundum quam omnia dogmata omnesque doctores aestimari et iudicari oporteat, nullam omnino aliam esse quam prophetica et apostolica scripta tum Veteris tum Novi Testamenti. . . .": "Formula Concordiae, Epitome Articulorum. De compendiaria regula atque norma," in *Die Bekenntnisschriften der evangelisch-lutherischen Kirche* (Berlin, ⁵1960) 767.

[37] *Denz.* 1507; 3018 and 3020; 3884.

cupies in the Church, the privileges with which she has been invested by her Son, and our duties toward her, this explanation being based on the documents of the magisterium" (n. 1).

In the *Praenotanda* accompanying the schema the authors rightly describe the text as "the teaching of the ecclesiastical magisterium" (n. 3). They also consider it fitting to establish the grounds for their decision: there exist among theologians, they say, controversies about the origin, authority and meaning of the sources of Christian tradition; the authors are therefore right to lean on the authority of the Church's magisterium alone; the certainty of the doctrine which it teaches has been guaranteed by the special help of the Holy Spirit, so that it is proper to interpret even scripture and the Fathers in accordance with the explanations of this magisterium.[38]

In fact the schema presented for the approval of the fathers was largely composed of the express or indirectly reported utterances of the sovereign pontiffs, particularly Pius XII. The text and notes refer 117 times to papal declarations, as opposed to 57 citations of scripture (including parallelisms) and 30 of the Fathers. One Protestant theologian summed up the method followed in this schema in a phrase which is no doubt exagger-

---

[38] "III. Hic illic remittitur ad quōsdam fontes traditionis christianae. Attenta autem controversia inter theologos catholicos circa originem, auctoritatem et sensum talium fontium, hoc Schema opportune non singulis dictis sive Patrum sive theologorum, sed ipsius Magisterii Ecclesiae auctoritate nititur, cuius doctrinae certitudo a speciali assistentia Spiritus Sancti provenit, ita ut ad sensum huius Magisterii et Scriptura et Patres interpretandi sunt. Neque silentio praetereundum ipsum quoque Pium XII, in Litteris Encyclicis Ad Caeli Reginam (cf. *AAS* 46 [1954] 628) allegare maxime discussa opera S. EPHRAEM, nempe Hymnos et Orationes, minime sane volens ideo dare, ut dicitur, 'garantiam' authenticitati talium operum. Unde potius quam singulae notas (hic a nobis interim, seu ad tempus positae, et quae habent secundarium momentum) singulae propositiones schematis, in quibus nullum novum dogma, et ex ipso schemate clare apparet, sed solida et sana *doctrina Magisteri ecclesiastici* (my italics) prostat, sedulo ponderandae et examini subiciendae sunt." Schema Constitutionum et Decretarum de quibus disceptabitur in Concilii sessionibus, series secunda, De Ecclesia et de B. Maria Virgine, *Typis Polyglottis Vaticanis* 1962, 99-100.

ated but certainly expressive: "Denzinger has beaten the Gospel." [39]

The chapter *De Beata* which was finally accepted departs substantially from the method just mentioned. The fathers, preoccupied with ecumenism, demanded categorically that the schema should be given a more biblical character. The task was by no means easy. The method of the first schema certainly seemed to rest on unshakable foundations; was it not regarded as legitimate, indeed, almost obligatory, in Catholic theology? Moreover, not without significance was the fact that it corresponded with the views of a sizeable fraction of mariologians and Council fathers who thought to enhance Mary's glory by constantly giving her new titles and proclaiming her new privileges as obligatory Catholic doctrine.[40] It is clear that the pontifical documents provided them with more arguments with which to support their suggestions than the pages of the Gospel did. In addition, the shifting of the accent from scripture awoke grave fears that mariology would thereby be impoverished and lose the ground that it had won during the course of centuries. However, the biblical renewal gained a notable success.[41] The Virgin Mary was shown in the context of the economy of salvation. The text of Galatians 4, 4 and the Apocalypse, which situate Mary in the divine plan, provided the framework for the new presentation. The privileges of our Lord's Mother were formulated to a large extent in simple words taken straight from scripture. No attempt has been made in this Chapter VIII to pass over in discreet silence the so-called anti-Marian texts. Interpretation of the biblical quotations is reduced to a minimum. The mariology of Chapter VIII has been thereby to a certain extent impoverished, but in return it has acquired tre-

[39] D. Fernandez, "Fundamentos patrísticos del capítulo VIII de la Constitución 'Lumen Gentium'," in *Ephemerides Mariologicae* 16 (1966) 75.

[40] More than 400 fathers were in favor of the proclamation of a new dogma on Mary: 300 wanted her mediation of all graces, 50 the coredemption, 50 her spiritual motherhood, and 20 her royal dignity and authority. Cf. R. Laurentin, *La Vierge au Concile* (Paris, 1965) 9.

[41] *Ibid.,* 57.

mendous conviction. In the last analysis, the quantitative im-
poverishment of mariology has been balanced by a qualitative
enrichment; mariology has become more catholic: henceforth it
is better fitted to become the common property of the whole of
Christendom. Pontifical utterances have yielded to the biblical
view. Of the 117 citations from pontifical documents in the
text and notes of the original schema only 14 remain in the
final text of this chapter. This change in the presentation of
doctrine on the Virgin Mary seems to open up vast possibilities
in the field of mariology for a Catholic-Protestant dialogue.

III

THE PROBLEM OF THE MEDIATION OF MARY

The mediation of Mary was studied with great attention by
Catholic theologians in the period preceding the Council. When
J. Carol was preparing a monograph on the co-redemption of
Mary he enumerated more than 3,000 authors who had written
on the subject before 1950;[42] the period from 1921 to 1958
alone saw the appearance of more than 300 works directly devoted to the study of the co-redemption.[43] Writers laid much
emphasis on the universal character of the dispensation of graces
by Mary: all graces, it was asserted, came through Mary's
hands, in the sense that we owe all divine favors to the special
intervention of the Mother of God. These propositions were
usually supported by quotations from theologians, saints and
popes. The exponents of Mary's direct cooperation in the objective fact of redemption became ever more numerous and
strove to establish the thesis that Mary, together with Christ,
earned the treasures of the redemption *de congruo* and even *de
condigno*. Numerous theologians mentioned, as Mary's princi-

[42] Cf. J. B. Carol, *De corredemptione B.V.M. Disquisitio positiva*
(Vatican City, 1950) 9.
[43] Cf. G. Baraúna, *De natura corredemptionis Marianae in theologia
hodierna* (1921-1958). *Disquisitio expositivo-critica* (Rome, 1960)
XIII-XXVIII.

pal co-redemptive acts, her sufferings and her surrender of her maternal rights over Christ.[44]

Protestant theologians consider that in loyalty to the biblical message they must reject a Catholic mariology conceived in these terms. After excluding the possibility of any collaboration of man with God in the work of justification, they are obliged to utter a resolute "no" to what they hear from the Catholic side about the mediation of Mary. Pre-conciliar Protestant theology noted that the very words of the Gospel indicated that Mary had not always understood her Son,[45] who in any case explicitly denied any fellowship with his Mother on the level of his messianic mission.[46] Contemporary Protestantism rejects the principle of a close union between Mary and Christ in the work of redemption and champions on the contrary the principle of a complete separation between Christ and any of those he has redeemed, including Mary. It is true that one also sometimes hears Protestants speaking of the exceptional intimacy between Mary and Christ [47] and of her participation in the work of redemption;[48] but these and other similar statements must be interpreted in the light of Protestant theology as a whole, which firmly rejects any active collaboration on the part of a creature in the work of redemption carried out by Christ. According to Protestant theologians, one can only speak of an active participation by Mary in the work of redemption in the sense in which

[44] Cf. *ibid.*, I et III.

[45] W. Grundmann, *Die Geschichte Jesu Christi* (Berlin, 1956) 400; A. Oepke, "Das Dogma von der Himmelfarht Maria in Lichte des Neuen Testaments und der früchristlichen Uberlieferung," in *Evangelisch-lutherische Kirchenzeitung* 5 (1951) 106.

[46] G. Neefe, *Maria unterwegs. Ein Bild der Mutter Jesu nach den biblischen Berichten* (Berlin, 1959) 21-23; W. Künneth, "Thesen zur Mariologie," in *Evangelische Welt* 5 (1950) 581; H. Lamparter, *op. cit.*, 16; E. Rudolph, *Jesu Mutter nach dem Verständnis der evangelisch-lutherischen Kirche* (Berlin, 1958) 27; A. Schlatter, *Marien-Reden* (Gladbeck in Westfalen, ³1951) 43; H. Roux, *op. cit.*, 83; "Maria," in *Lexikon zur Bibel* (ed. F. Rienecker) (Wuppertal, 1960) 886.

[47] W. Meyer, *op. cit.*, 585; W. Stählin, *op. cit.*, 748.

[48] H. Lamparter, *op. cit.*, 20.

the Apostle wrote that he supplied in his flesh what was missing from the sufferings of Christ.[49]

The title "Co-redemptrix" meets extremely strong opposition from Protestants.[50] To grant Mary the dignity of Co-redemptrix is, they think, to place her by the side of Christ.[51] P. Bourguet[52] points out that if there is a Co-redemptrix by the side of Christ, this means in effect that he himself is only a Co-redeemer. By the incarnation and the toil of his earthly life the Word has made himself so much ours, so near and immediately accessible, that to seek a mediator between such a mediator and men becomes blasphemy and a negation of the reality of the incarnation: such are the stern reproaches they sometimes address to us. They ask us if Christ is too much God and too little man for us to be able to approach him directly, so that we need more merciful and more human intermediaries.[53] H. Asmussen expresses the disquiet of the Protestant spirit in the face of Catholic teaching on the mediation of Mary in this way: "One would think that Jesus Christ is not enough. Between him and us you put the Virgin Mary." [54]

It could not be expected that the Council would demolish the dividing wall formed by the doctrine of the mediation of Mary. Nonetheless, the Council has kindled many hopes. Chapter VIII is far-reaching in what it says as well as in what it leaves unsaid. And it leaves a great deal unsaid. Its silence cannot be interpreted as a cheap dialectical trick. The Council could not leave out points of doctrine essential to the subject under discussion,

[49] G. Miegge, *La Vergine Maria. Saggio di storia del dogma* (Torre Pellice, 1950) 199 and 201.

[50] H. Lamparter, *op. cit.*, 24.

[51] "Hirtenbrief des Bischofs der Evangelischen Kirche Augsburgischen Bekennthisses in Osterreich, Dr. Gehrard May," in *Oekumenische Einheit* 2 (1951) 86.

[52] *Op. cit.*, 27-28.

[53] The expression "mediation by stages" is used by J. Hamer in the article "Mariologie et théologie protestante," in *Divus Thomas* 55 (1952) 366.

[54] H. Asmussen, "Dem Unbefleckten Herzen Mariä geweiht?" in *Gloria Dei* 9 (1954) 207.

especially those which would immediately have to be dealt with on the very threshold of the ecumenical encounter.

We should first note the omission of the title "Co-redemptrix". The authors of the first schema had justified abandoning it on ecumenical grounds, while including in the titles the most genuine ones.[55] The schema accepts the omission without an explanatory note of any kind. It calls Mary *Advocata, Auxiliatrix, Adjutrix* and *Mediatrix,* but it restricts the meaning of these terms in such a way that they become acceptable in unprejudiced Protestant circles. Section 62 of *Lumen Gentium* explains these titles as indicating intercession. It is thus not so much the problem of intercession as such which divides the two Churches as the fact of imploring the assistance of Mary and the saints. And in fact when one prays to the saints and to Mary it is to them that one turns and not to Christ; this impairs the direct, affectionate, personal relationship binding the redeemed to his redeemer.

In the second place, the Council has left out a number of expressions introduced by the popes and particularly wounding to Protestant susceptibilities, such as that of *Reparatrix totius orbis* (Leo XIII) and Pius X's view that Mary has earned *de congruo* all that Christ has earned *de condigno.* Nor does the chapter *De Beata* make use of the terminology current among theologians when they are discussing the nature of Mary's active participation in the accumulation of the treasures of the redemption: objective redemption, subjective redemption, merit *de congruo* and *de condigno,* and so on. This terminology in fact, and the concepts bound up with it, was bottling up discussion of Mary's role in the work of redemption in a dead end.[56]

---

[55] *Praenotanda* IV, 3a.

[56] A. Müller points out that mariology, though Catholic at the point of departure, is not necessarily Catholic at the point of arrival; he then explains how it can finish up in a dead end: "Trotzdem gibt es such in der heutigen Theologie mariologische Positionen, die entweder in der Tendenz oder in den Formulierung, meist dann in beiden, nicht zu gesunden Entwicklung führen, sondern in Sackgasse, zu Endpunkten. Von solchen Erscheinungen müsste sich die katholische Theologie reinigen, selbst wenn das mariologische kein ökumenisches Problem wäre.

Another important factor is what the Council did not say about the universal dispensation of graces. *De Beata* makes no mention of the dispensation of all grace through the intercession of Mary, although theologians have given this thesis a very high theological rating.[57] This omission possesses far-reaching ecumenical importance, since none of the proposition's defenders was in a position to buttress it on scripture.

Another omission from Chapter VIII is of great significance for the dialogue between Catholics and Protestants: there is no mention of a mediatrix by the side of the mediator. This idea of mediation in stages was formulated by St. Bernadine of Sienna and adopted word-for-word by Leo XIII.[58] The omission seems to have been conscious and intentional indeed, for the text finally adopted emphasizes that the mediation of Mary in no way forms an obstacle to the direct union of the faithful with Christ (n. 61). *De Beata* does not explain the problem thoroughly; it does not say how we are to reconcile the doctrine of the mediation of Mary with direct union with Christ. The first schema proposed to resolve this difficulty by replacing the idea of mediating with the mediator by that of mediation in Christ. It was apparently the first time that this proposition had been formulated in the Church's teaching. It was not employed in the text finally adopted. If I am not mistaken, it originated among the Protestants; it was in H. Asmussen that I first saw it clearly formulated.[59] It was taken up on the Catholic side by

---

Denn die katholische Lehre muss ja auch in sich und zuerst in sich im Gleichgewicht und auf einer gesunden Linie bleiben": A. Müller, Ökumenische Orientierung der katholischen Mariologie," in *Freiburger Zeitschrift für Philosophie und Theologie* 12 (1965) 86.

[57] Cf. G. Roschini, *Mariologia* II (Rome, ²1947) 397.

[58] Enc. *Iucunda semper*, in H. Marin, *Documentos marianos* (Madrid, 1954) 289.

[59] "Wenn das so ist, dann müssen wir aber auch anerkennen, dass Maria in dieser Mittlerschaft steht, weil sie ein vornehmes Glied der priesterlichen Schar ist. Die Frage ist nur—bei der Mutter Gottes ebenso wie bei allen anderen Christen—, ob es sich um eine Mittlerschaft *in* Christus oder um eine Mittlerschaft *neben* Christus handelt. Denn dies ist offensichtlich die Unterscheidung, an welcher nicht weniger als alles hängt. Kennen wir eine Mittlerschaft neben Christus, dann ist die Ehre Christi wirklich angefochten. Rechnen wir aber mit einer Mittlerschaft

H. Fries.[60] Its insertion in the first schema shows that it enjoys great esteem among serious Catholic theologians; it also bears witness to the realization of Protestant disquiet.

Chapter VIII formulates a series of reservations about the meaning to be given to the mediation of Mary, pointing out in particular that it does not obscure the sole mediation of Christ but reveals its strength; that the Virgin's saving influence on men does not flow from the nature of things but from the free divine choice and the superabundance of the merits of Christ; and that it rests on the mediation of the latter, on which it is entirely dependent for all its efficacy. It is worth paying special attention to two comparisons which show in a simple, convincing and biblical way that there is no disharmony between the eminent part played by Mary in the work of redemption and the words of 1 Timothy 2, 5 about the sole mediator. According to *De Beata,* the mediatory function of creatures in the economy of salvation does not exclude the uniqueness of the mediation of Christ any more than the priesthood of the faithful is in opposition to the unique priesthood of Christ, or than the goodness scattered in various degrees in creatures infringes the unique goodness of God. The analogy drawn from the priesthood of Christ and that of the faithful deserves to be specially noted for it is close, comprehensible and exceptionally dear to Protestant hearts. Starting from the comparison established between mediation on the one hand and priesthood and goodness on the

der Christen *in* Christus, dann sagen wir damit aus, dass Christi Werk nicht fruchtlos geblieben ist. Haben wir dagegen einen Christus, der wohl als der einige Mittler anerkannt wird, dem man es aber abspricht, dass sein Mittlertum die Frucht trug, dass andere in dies Mittlertum eintreten und seine Mitarbeiter wurden, dann müssen wir uns auch fragen lassen, ob wir nicht seiner Ehre empfindlich Abtrag tun. Daraus entsteht dann die Frage, ob wir anerkennen, dass Maria, die Mutter des Herrn, nicht nur ihn als seine irdische Mutter hervorbrachte, sondern auch in seinem Reiche zu seiner Jüngerin wurde, die in seiner Nachfolge teilnimmt an seinem Mittlertum. Bejahen wir dieses Frage, dann wäre damit allerdings noch nicht geklärt, ob diese Teilnahme in der römischen Lehrausprägung und im römischen Gottesdienst in rechten Weise zum Ausdruck käme." The phrases underlined are given in italics by Asmussen in *Maria, die Mutter Gottes* (Stuttgart, 1950) 51.

[60] *Antwort an Asmussen* (Stuttgart, 1958) 132.

other, the Council affirms that the unique mediation of Christ is the source whence creatures draw their mediatory office. It is interesting to note that the first schema had formulated this idea in a much more concise way. It had in fact rested content with mentioning that the sole mediation of Christ did not exclude the mediation of Mary any more than the goodness of Mary contradicted the truth that God alone is good (n. 63). The text adopted by the fathers has retained the analogy between mediation and goodness and added that of the priesthood. It looks as if the concept proposed will do much to facilitate the dialogue between Protestants and Catholics on the crucial problem of mediation.

IV

THE PROBLEM OF MARIAN DEVOTION

Catholic veneration of the Virgin Mary has two aspects, liturgical and extra-liturgical, or private. From the liturgical point of view, three elements seem to occupy the foreground: *commemoration, salutation* and *invocation*.

Mention of Mary. We recall passages of scripture which speak of her or, more briefly, we evoke what she was, who she was and what function she fulfilled. This second kind of mention is employed in prayers.[61]

There is a similar commemoration in the canon of the Mass at the *Communicantes.*

We pray to God, Christ. The commemoration of Mary is an opportunity to direct our thoughts toward "all-powerful and eternal God" or his "only Son". The theocentrism and christocentrism of such a concept are strikingly obvious.

Salutation of Mary. From the first half of the 4th century onward joyous salutations to the Mother of God were introduced into the liturgy (the *Ave Maria,* etc.).

Invocation of Mary. The liturgical invocation of the Virgin is chronologically a later element than the two previous ones.

---

[61] Collecte de la messe pour le 25 mars.

It is interesting to note that in the proper of Masses for the feasts of Mary it is not to her, as a general rule, that we address ourselves to solicit her intervention, but to God, asking him to hear our prayers through the intercession of Mary.

However, it does sometimes happen, especially in the more recent strata of the liturgy, that we turn directly to the Virgin Mary to ask her either to intercede for us or to do something in our favor.

Extra-liturgical Marian devotion is considerably less concerned about being theocentric and christocentric. The exchanges take place rather between the soul or the community at prayer and the person of Mary, without explicit reference to God or Christ. The psychological element occupies the foreground: Mary is reminded that she is our Mother, that she is good, that she must help, that she must understand. The phrase "Pray for us" recurs frequently and "Pray" sometimes gives way to stronger words such as "Give", "Do", "Charge" which are absent from the classical liturgy.

This extra-liturgical devotion lays exceptional emphasis on Mary's maternal mercy toward us; it recalls that her Son, while he is merciful, must remain a just judge.

When we came to the Protestant position on the question of the veneration of Mary, it should be noted that only in appearance is it unanimous and concordant. No complete hagiology is to be found in the *Confession of Augsburg*, the *Apologia for the Confession of Augsburg*, the *Articles of Smalkalde* or any other confessional documents of the Protestant Churches. The affirmations we find there cannot be reduced in any way to a common denominator.[62] Contemporary Protestant theologians resolutely reject Catholic forms of Marian devotion, but they are not certain whether a cult of the Mother of our Lord exists in their Churches. Some think that it does,[63] others incline to believe

---

[62] Cf. M. Lackmann, *Verehrung der Heiligen* (Stuttgart, 1958) 27; W. Tanner, "Maria, die Mutter," in *Kirchenblatt für Reformierte Schweiz* 111 (1955) 145.

[63] ". . . il y a un motif pour bénir Marie": H. Lamparter, *op. cit.*, 7. W. Künneth considers that there can exist a fashion, correctly under-

that it does not,[64] the latter being much more numerous. As a general rule the two concepts of dulia and hyperdulia are rejected as illegitimate. Protestants can commemorate the Mother of our Lord, and they are in fact doing this more and more frequently and openly. The Protestant is thus in principle free to believe that the Virgin Mary intercedes for us. A more thorny problem is that of invocation, which is unacceptable to most Protestants, who see in it an infringement of the honor due to Christ. They protest energetically against the profusion of extra-liturgical forms of Marian devotion, claiming that these are related to pagan and superstitious practices.[65] It seems that these

---

stood, of blessing Mary which must be described as a cult. W. Künneth, "Evangelische Mariologie?" in *Evangelisch-lutherische Kirchenzeitung* 5 (1951) 8. W. Tanner declares: "If it is a question for Catholics of honoring the Mother of the Lord, we are with them": W. Tanner, *Maria, die Mutter*, 145.

[64] To the question "What place does Mary occupy in the piety of the Reformed Church?" Pastor Roux replies: "She holds no place": H. Roux, *op. cit.*, 89. Before moving over to Catholicism, T. Grin, although he had perceived the positive values of the Catholic Marian cult, considered that he could not be associated with it if he was to remain loyal to the truth professed in the Reformed Church: T. Grin, "Prédication prononcée à Constance, à l'église française, le premier dimanche de l'Avent 1950," in *Le Monde Religieux* 32-33 (1950) 88. G. Miegge (†1961), professor at the Institute of Torre Pellice (Vaud), was of the opinion that for us Mary is simply the sweet earthly mother of Jesus and does not deserve to be paid great honor. Cf. G. Miegge, "Intorno al Dogma dell'assunzione: I. Theologia e simbolo nel culto della Vergine Maria. II. L'Enciclica 'Munificentissimus Deus'", in *Protestantesimo* 6 (1951) 43. J. Weerda says that the Reformation rejects the formal veneration of Mary: J. Weerda, "Mariologia," in *Die Religion in Geschichte und Gegenwart* IV (Tübingen, 1960) 769. It seems that the statements of Protestant theologians about the existence or non-existence of veneration for Mary in their Church are contradictory only in appearance. A more careful analysis of the text and context discloses that those theologians who are opposed to the cult of Mary are in fact protesting against Catholic forms of the cult of the Virgin; as for those who seem to recognize the legitimacy of the cult of Mary, they do not in any way share the Catholic point of view about it, for they understand this cult in their own ways, which in any case are not always uniform.

[65] Cf. K. Nitzschke, *op. cit.*, 1250; R. Mehl, *op. cit.*, 87-88; G. Miegge, *La Vergine Maria*, 86-89; F. Heiler, "Marienverehrung, I. In der kath. Kirche," in *Die Religion in Geschichte und Gegenwart* IV (Tübingen, 1960) 765; A. Oepke, *op. cit.*, 105; J. Amstutz, "Die Ve-

extra-liturgical practices do much more to deter Protestants from paying homage to our Lord's Mother than considerations of a theological nature.

Of the cult of the Mother of God, Chapter VIII says quite simply that it is a "special" cult (n. 66).[66] Secondly, in its recommendations for the development of the Marian cult, Chapter VIII gives a certain priority to the liturgical forms.[67] It seems that the degree to which the extra-liturgical cult of Mary is harmonized with the liturgical cult will affect in turn the degree of ecumenical reconciliation. In the third place, the chapter *De Beata* adopts the repeated warnings of Pius XII and John XXIII to theologians and preachers to be on their guard not only against excessive timidity when they speak of the Most Holy Virgin but also against excessive exaggeration in considering her position as the Mother of God (n. 67). Fourthly, the last chapter of *Lumen Gentium* recommends prudence in the choice of devotional practices. The lack, apparent or real, of this prudence turns away our Protestant brethren from those very forms of veneration for our Lord's Mother which are in conformity with Protestant orthodoxy. We must take care, says the *Constitution*, that our separated brethren, seeing the way in which we express our love for the Mother of Christ, do not make false inferences about the real nature of Catholic doctrine (n. 67). The tragedy of 1517 was in fact at the start a revolt against concrete manifestations of the Church's life; the doctrinal break only occurred later. M. Lackmann, who possesses the gift of being able to express himself in striking imagery, assures us that "the lonely God" of Protestantism, "the deserted heaven" and

---

rehrung Marias vom freien Protestantismus gesehen," in *Eine Heilige Kirche* 1 (1955-1956) 40-41; P. Bourguet, *La Vierge Marie, Écriture et tradition* (Paris, ²1956) 24; E. G. Rüsch, *Wir Protestanten und Maria* (St. Gallen, 1951) 23-24.

[66] Section 3 of the Constitution on the *Sacred Liturgy* says that the Church venerates Mary with a special love: "In hoc annuo mysteriorum Christi circulo celebrando, sancta Ecclesia beatam Mariam Dei Genetricem cum peculiari amore veneratur. . . ."

[67] ". . . sacrosancta synodus consulto docet, simulque omnes Ecclesiae filios admonet, ut *cultum, praesertim liturgicum* (my italics), erga beatam Virginem generose foveat. . . ." (No. 67).

the severe "asceticism" in the cult of the saints are closely linked to Protestantism's perception of abuses in Catholicism.[68] The wishes formulated by the Council put pastoral theology before the difficult, infinitely delicate, yet necessary task of revising the existing forms of the Marian cult.[69]

To sum up the foregoing remarks, we can say that the chapter *De Beata* attempts to show Mary from four aspects: biblical, christocentric, ecclesiotypical and liturgical. In the ecumenical dialogue it is no doubt the *biblical* aspect which is the most important. Deductive mariology seemed to rest on such solid foundations that the reaction of the various different theologians was to some extent prejudiced in advance; great courage and the highest authority were required in order to surmount it. As for the *christocentric* aspect, it ought to orientate theological thinking toward the attempt to harmonize the function of the sole mediator with the mediation of Mary, an attempt which it has been agreed to call "the concept of participation". The *ecclesiotypical* aspect, to which Chapter VIII gives an important place, situates the Virgin more explicitly on the side of redeemed humanity, facing with it the common redeemer. The *liturgical* aspect has given to mariology, as well as to Marian devotion, the important task of going back to the healthiest sources of Christian thought.

Christian theology is not a closed theology but a theology in motion. Chapter VIII of *Lumen Gentium* marks out the guidelines for an indispensable reconsideration of the route hitherto followed in mariology; the new torches which the Council has kindled must enable mariology to play a fuller part in the attainment of unity.

---

[68] M. Lackmann, *op. cit.*, 47. Cf. also R. Schimpfennig, *Die Geschichte der Marienverehrung im deutschen Protestantismus* (Paderborn, 1952) 125.

[69] Cf. V. Noè, "Le devozioni mariane in armonia con la liturgia," in *La Madonna nel culto della Chiesa*, 274-300; D. M. Montagna, *op. cit.*, 9-33; F. I. Elizari, "Pastoral Mariana a la luz del capitolo sobre la Virgen," in *Ephemerides Mariologicae* 16 (1966) 162-187; A. Müller, "Piété mariale et éducation de la foi," in *Etudes Mariales* 21 (1964) 95-105; R. Laurentin, *La question mariale* (Paris, 1963) tr.: *Mary's Place in the Church* (London and New York, 1965) *passim*.

PART III
DOCUMENTATION
CONCILIUM

Office of the Executive Secretary
Nijmegen, Netherlands

Georg Siegmund / *Fulda-Neuenberg, West Germany*

The Encounter with Buddhism

I

THE ONSET OF DIALOGUE

We have passed from a time for drawing boundaries to a time for listening to each other. In recent years the Church has made a new beginning and this has given both theologians and faithful new work to perform. This work includes the opening of the door to non-Christians. Our world is becoming more and more of a unit; the fate of one nation cannot be isolated from the fate of its neighbors. A threat to one nation is a threat to mankind, and our common situation encourages us to lay aside our differences and work together for the common good.

It is surely providential that the character of Pope John XXIII and Vatican Council II itself gave new life to the encounter between East and West. What was unthinkable before is now happening. In the largest bookshop in the largest city in the world—Tokyo with its 14 million inhabitants—*Pacem in Terris,* the encyclical of Pope John XXIII, is a best seller. This humanly admirable pope succeeded where conferences on world views and official doctrinal definitions failed. He gave the word "brotherly" a new and more hopeful connotation. His brotherly behavior to men of all races and religions did more to open men's hearts than any proclamation. In November, 1962 he gave an audience to 30 Japanese Buddhists of various sects in his private library.

The Buddhists asked for this audience to speak to the head of the largest Christian Church about working together for world peace.

We do not know exactly what the pope said, but we know what impression he made on his visitors. The leader of the group, the Zen Abbot Iwamoto, told Heinrich Dumoulin, professor of Oriental religions at Sophia University in Tokyo, that their conversation surprised and delighted them. They had imagined that the pope would thank them for their visit and then explain that Christianity was the highest religion and all men must adopt it. Instead the pope was respectful to their religion and more or less said that belief in God and belief in Buddha had the same foundation, and that all religious people should work together in peace for the good of mankind.

By no word did he suggest that he was superior to them, and this confirmed them in their resolution to disregard their sectarian differences and work together for the common good. The Buddhist abbot went on to speak enthusiastically of the events of the rest of the day. The pope shook hands with each of them and gave to each a silver medal inscribed with his portrait.[1]

The contact established between the Japanese Buddhists and the pope has been maintained. In the autumn of 1966 Pope Paul VI received 15 Japanese bonzes. The pope replied to their speaker's address by a brief speech, stating his happiness that the numerous recent visits of Japanese Buddhists had created a relationship of goodwill and respect between Buddhism and the Catholic Church. Because world peace was in danger, the pope said, all religious people should work together to create circumstances favorable to that peace which we all desire. In conclusion he expressed his hope that their visit would contribute to that spirit of tolerance and mutual respect aroused by the Council and strengthen the part played by religion in furthering the good of mankind and the education of the human family.[2]

[1] Heinrich Dumoulin, *Ostliche Meditation und christliche Mystik* (Freiburg/Munich, 1966), p. 35.

[2] Cf. "Japanische Bonzen beim Papst (Kurznachrichten aus Kirche und Welt)" in *Die Kirche nach dem Konzil* 12 (Cologne, 1966), p. 1.

This personal contact and recognition already presupposes that each accepts the other as "religious", and this is by no means a self-evident truth. There are Buddhists who would place Buddhism on quite a different plane from Christianity because of Buddhism's apersonalism and atheism,[3] and there are Christian scholars who regard Buddhism as a world-view but not as a religion.

In Vatican Council II's *Declaration on Non-Christian Religions* (October 28, 1965), Buddhism is spoken of as follows: "In its various forms Buddhism recognizes the radical insufficiency of this changing world and teaches a way by which pious and faithful people can be perfectly set free, or, either by their own action or by help from above, can reach the highest state of enlightenment." The way is thus prepared for dialogue, a dialogue that will not seek to draw boundaries but to reach mutual understanding and to come closer together through this understanding.

When people who have long lived side by side in silence suddenly begin to talk, in their first delight at the encounter they may overemphasize what they have in common and forget what divides them. This often happens with Christians who begin to explore Buddhism. At first they notice many similarities with Christianity. The value placed on reverence, the calls to prayer, methods of contemplation, the cult of the dead, use of incense, candles, forms of prayer, the practice of meditation and going on pilgrimages, the honor paid to great masters of contemplation and ascesis—all this gives to the uninformed an impression of great inner similarity.

But closer study reveals the radical difference. For example, a commentator on Nishida Kitaro who is thought to be the

[3] Cf. Kurt Schmidt, *Buddha's Lehre, Eine Einführung* (Constance, 1946), p. 9.: "The doctrine which Buddha bequeathed mankind knows no divine creator and ruler of the world, no savior, no divine revelation, no soul—if by soul one means a changeless essence—and no religious dogmas which man must believe in order to attain his highest goal which is eternal peace. On the contrary, Buddha warned against accepting religious dogmas on any authority. Is it then possible to call Buddhism a religion? No, it is not in the usual sense of the word."

greatest philosopher in Japan explains as follows: "It is peculiar to the East to regard nothingness as the ground of all existence. To the West this is mysterious, to the East it is a commonplace. . . . The idea of absolute nothingness is perhaps the hardest to understand for the Western reader; in the East it is the most usual way of thinking. In Western religion God is the highest existence, and, commonly speaking, the ground of existence is existence itself. In Mahayaba Buddhism in the East, on the other hand, to cling to existence is simply ignorance." [4]

In other words, "absolute nothingness" is made into a metaphysical principle which is the ground of all being but is not itself being. If nothingness has the metaphysical function of being the last resting place of all being, this appears expressly to contradict the Christian doctrine which ascribes this function to God, and this makes the Christian feel that the ground has been taken away from under his feet. The friend of Francis Xavier Cosmas de Torres clearly felt this in discussions with Zen monks. He said in a letter that these men, so advanced in spirituality by their long contemplation, would ask him questions that Thomas Aquinas or Duns Scotus would have found hard to answer.

The Buddhist side continually stresses that the fundamental principle for Buddhism is really "absolute nothingness". If this were so, there could be nothing to relate it to Christianity. It serves no worthwhile purpose when the Western side repeatedly tries to prove that they are deceiving themselves: that they do not mean "absolute nothingness" but "relative nothingness". This step would enable each side to take shelter in the security of their accustomed way of thinking and turn the "dialogue" into guerrilla expeditions from a safe base.

True dialogue can only be conducted from a mutually acceptable common base. This base must be really common and not merely appear to be so through ambiguous terminology.

It must be admitted that the difference between East and

[4] Cf. M. Heinrichs, *Katholische Theologie und asiatisches Denken* (Mainz, 1963), pp. 25f.

West is a radical one. Eastern thought is not metaphysical but soteriological, and the term "absolute nothingness" is used in a special sense. Eastern thought is primarily concerned with the attainment of "salvation" by suffering and sinful man, not with the grasping of the ground of being, for being has no ground. (Clearly the concept "ground of being" requires analysis.)

Forgetting for a moment the "otherness" of Eastern thought, we could say that it appears to be much nearer to Hegel with his dialectic which brings being out of nothingness, and to Heidegger with his invocation of nothingness, than to Christian thought per se. In fact both Hegel and Heidegger have a fascination for Japanese philosophy, and this is relevant to this philosophy's willingness to converse with the Christian.

Readiness to listen to the Christian is appreciably reduced by the flood of books on Zen Buddhism and Yoga which assume the bankruptcy of Christianity and offer salvation from the East. Most damage is done by the repeated assertion (which does not thereby gain in truth) that Western man through his activism has lost his awareness and his "soul" and must try to regain it through the Eastern teaching on salvation. The Buddhist and the Hindu are then liable to assume that a Christian who wants to talk to him must be a spiritual bankrupt wanting to discard the old and turn to something new. This has long been the effect of Schopenhauer's praise of Buddhism as a logical pessimism, whereas Christianity is an interrupted pessimism. Experienced missionaries who have striven for centuries to establish a true dialogue with the East do not have great hopes for the prospects of this dialogue.

Above all the otherness of Eastern thought must not be under-rated. The Western party is apt to conclude that in the East "the truth" is not very highly valued. He thinks with his emotions, expressly dislikes logical argument, denies the principle of contradiction, and resists analysis and the drawing of distinctions. He wants to think "as a whole person" in unity of thought and feeling, intellect and emotion. As the non-Christian religions do not require an intellectual or moral choice, it is assumed that one may turn from this to that "truth," to Shintoism, Buddhism, Hinduism or Christianity, as circumstances arise.

Even the value placed upon good and bad is not the same. The Eastern non-Christian tends like Goethe to see in evil a power which seeks evil but brings good. This relativizing of moral values sets at nought the Christian Gospel. Above all, Eastern wisdom does not have the notion of "sin" as absolute disvalue.

However, these severe difficulties should not discourage the desire for true dialogue. The first dialogue may do no more than make each party explicitly aware of his own position. But this would be the necessary preliminary to any further progress.

II

THE BASIC BUDDHIST EXPERIENCE

Christianity begins with the person of Jesus of Nazareth who was called Christ, and Buddhism with Siddhartha Gautama who was called Buddha. On closer inspection these facts reveal a fundamental difference in the origins of the two religions. Jesus Christ taught his message of salvation not merely as a doctrine, but announced himself as the bringer of salvation and the way. Buddha, however, merely taught a doctrine—salvation through enlightenment, which each man can attain by himself. The amazing spread of his teaching throughout the Far East and the fact that many nations have adopted Buddhism and have not been afraid to develop it and build around it connected the deepest experiences and thought processes of these nations. No one in the East regards the breaking away from origins as a "falling away", as Christians do when attempts are made to separate "Christianity" from "Jesus Christ". The continuity principle in Buddhism, as Maurus Heinrichs says,[5] is not faithfulness to the historical Buddha but the common experience and view of life of Eastern man. Modern Buddhist sects that no longer regard the historical Siddhartha Gautama as essential to their

[5] *Op cit.*, p. 33.

religion, but think of him as a general Buddha-Nature (Chinese: *fo-hsing;* Japanese: *buss-ho*) do not regard this as a falling away but as a legitimate development in accordance with the mind of the founder.

It is necessary to remember this different position of the founder of Buddhism in order to give the rightful place to Buddha's original experience, which is the basis of Buddhism. Philological and archeological sources have now established that the man to whom the foundation of Buddhism is ascribed really lived.[6] However, the historical facts of his life were very early overlaid with legend which we can no longer satisfactorily remove. It is not the historical details which are important, but the typical Buddha-experience, which appealed to Eastern man and which the Buddhist disciple tries to experience for himself by his contemplation so that he may be enlightened like his master.

Buddhism did not arise from a material or spiritual need; it was not a political movement or a movement to reform a decadent religion. Its root lies in a bourgeois satiety which is not interested in the satisfaction of needs or in appealing to the heroic side of human nature.

Self-consciousness of a personal identity can only be gained by fighting and overcoming difficulties. The East forgot this and was thus able to conceive of the human person as compounded of elements—spiritual and material elements, personal and eternal elements. The material elements guaranteed his death. "The personal and eternal element is the changing, and may be called the self (*atman*), the vital principle (*jiva*) or the man (*purusa*), etc. This eternal and changing element is denied by the materialistic sects because according to them man consists only of material and perishable elements and ceases with his death. For these sects there was therefore no problem of salvation." [7] Brah-

[6] Cf. Andre Bareau, "Der indische Buddhismus," in *Die Religionen Indiens* (Stuttgart), p. 11.

[7] *Op. cit.,* p. 9.

manism had been the cause of a deep seated pessimism when it taught that the fault for the world's fall was Brahman's, the primal being.

Even though Buddha's life is so lost in legend, his original experience is on the whole reported without much divergence and all sects take it as their starting point. Gautama was the son of a "prince" and born in India in the 6th century before Christ. His mother who wanted to visit her parents before her confinement gave birth to him unexpectedly on her journey and died soon afterward. The boy was given the first name Siddhartha; his surname Gautama is the name of a Vedic seer. The name Buddha, by which he was later called, is a title like "Messiah" for Jesus or "Prophet" for Mohammed. The word "Buddha" means "Awakened" or "Enlightened One".

Tradition is probably correct in telling that Gautama was brought up by his mother's sister, was raised in comfort, and married his cousin Yashodhara. Other women's names suggest that he had several wives. His father protected him from the knowledge of suffering; he wanted his son to be a great ruler and not an ascetic who renounced the world, as the holy Asita had prophesied. But the father's care was in vain. On several journeys the young man saw old people who had been abandoned, sick people, decaying corpses, and even ascetics. He was appalled by these sights and asked the driver what they meant. He was deeply moved by the explanation, but each time he returned home. On his return from his fourth journey he heard that a son had been born to him. He was very distressed and cried out: "Rahula is born to me; a chain has been forged for me." But this chain could not finally bind him to his home. He realized that all existence is suffering and this realization drove him away from home. One night he took silent leave of his sleeping wife and his newborn son and rode away, accompanied only by his faithful driver, to Anuvaieya, where he dismounted, laid aside his fine clothes, changed his silks for a hemp shirt, and sent back his companion to tell his grieving father and his heartbroken wife what he had done. He was twenty nine at the time.

This story has some confirmation in a traditional logion of the Buddha himself. He says: "When I lived in wealth and splendor I had the thought: When a worldly man, who is himself doomed to old age, sickness and death, looks at an old man or a sick man or a corpse, he is dismayed and appalled. Were I to be dismayed and appalled—I who was doomed to old age, sickness and death—at the sight of an old man, a sick man or a corpse, this would be wrong of me. With this thought all the pride of youth, all the pride of health and all the pride of life disappeared." [8]

Similarly, it is recounted in a biography of Buddha: "He who realizes the pain of the world by considering old age, sickness and death will be released from the pride he has fallen into in his power, his youth, his life." [9]

He studied yoga under two masters, whom he later praised, but it did not bring him the peace he wanted. He retired into solitude for several years and sought supernatural enlightenment by rigorous ascesis. At the end of his strength, he finally understood that this was not the way to attain his goal. He began to eat well again to cure his dangerous weakness. Under a tree, named by Buddhists the Bodhi tree—that is, the tree of enlightenment—he finally attained the enlightenment he had sought for so long: all life in all its forms is full of suffering; the origin of suffering is human desire; only by the destruction of desire and the extinction of all passion can suffering be stilled. The enlightenment contains nothing which was not already present in his first experience. Its distinguishing feature is that it gives the "nothingness" the status of a "principle" by which everything else is explained.

A proper understanding of Buddha's experience must place

[8] *Anguttara-Nikaya* III, 38, quoted by K. Schmidt, *Buddha's Lehre* (Constance, 1946), pp. 21f.

[9] *Das Leben des Buddha von Asvaghosa* (Tibetan and German version edited by Friedrich Weller) (Leipsig, 1926), p. 40.

it in the situation in which it occurred. It was a comfortable, even too comfortable world that he grew up in, a world which made no demands on the heroic side of his nature and which could not offer him the ideal of the hero magnificent in glorious deeds. Instead his father tried to preserve him from the knowledge of suffering.

However, suffering and the sensitivity to suffering have a curious relationship. He who tries to avoid the sufferings of life finds his sympathy with suffering growing immeasurably. In his flight from suffering, he is caught by suffering and its shadow throws him to the ground.

There have always been parents who have tried to keep from their children the suffering which they have endured and which has put its mark upon them; they want their children to have a better life than theirs. They do not understand that because of this correlation between suffering and sensitivity to suffering their efforts are in vain. Their children are not hardened by life but remain unprotected.

According to the stories of his life the young Gautama was the idol of his family and their rising hope. Such young men grow up assuming that they are special and have been set apart from the mass of "ordinary people", whose lot is suffering, age, death and meaninglessness even while they are alive. The pride of youth, the pride of health and the pride of life are the characteristics of the rich young man. He thinks he has a special claim on life because of his special position. The experience of nothingness, however, takes away this pride, and he understands that man of himself is absolutely nothing.

Foremost in Buddha's experience is this deep disappointment. Being the son of a prince he had not expected to be plunged into nothingness; he had expected a fortunate life, different from the common lot. But life on a bridge suspended over a precipice —a bridge which may break at any time and plunge its passenger into the abyss—was too much for his inexperienced and protected imagination. He was bitterly disappointed. Life to him, therefore, was simply "nothing".

The "fundamental truth" of Buddhism—that the world consists of suffering, and that therefore flight from the world is the
only proper course—is not basically an ontological statement or
an insight into the ontological status of the world. It is the outward projection of an inner experience, which thereby becomes
the quasi-principle by which everything in the world is explained
and valued. An excessive resentment declares that the "whole"
world consists of suffering and "only" suffering. This is why
Buddha's enlightenment must be seen in terms of his psychic
state and not as a logical or ontological statement about the
world.

It is proper here to examine the meaning of the word "disappointment". It is life which "disappoints" him who lives it.
Disappointment (German: *Enttäuschung*) comes from decep-
tion (*Täuschung*). Life must have "deceived" him—that is, not
given what it "promised". It is only possible to be disappointed
in previous expectations. He who had had none would not be
disappointed, and the greater the expectations, the more bitter
the disappointment. The sign of the most bitter disappointment
is to discount this life altogether.

Buddha's expectations are often spoken of in his biographies,
although they have no pretensions to psychological depth.
Buddha could not get over the thought that "everything is not
eternal". He was distressed by the thought that man must die,
and "without joy or fear": "When I realized that the world was
not eternal, my spirit had no more joy in it."

There is another reason for Buddha's experience of the nothingness of human life. The young man's developing powers
needed work to do. Doing work and achieving aims would have
filled the "empty", "nothing" life with content, meaning, value
and significance. A life which lacks aims cannot escape *taedium
vitae*. Research into suicide shows that aims can dispel *taedium
vitae*. Before World War II the very high suicide rate in Japan
was evidence of *taedium vitae*. When the war broke out, the
numbers—in other countries as well as Japan—decreased phe-
nomenally and continued to decrease at the rate of about ten

percent a year.[10] A collective faith—even when it later turns out to have been faith in a idol—induces people to make full use of their powers.

We now break off our analysis of Buddha's experience, but a further analysis of the concept *taedium vitae* may be useful.

III

CHRISTIAN AND BUDDHIST EXPERIENCE OF NOTHINGNESS

Buddha's experience is the experience of the absolute nothingness of man and the world. In his "enlightenment" this nothingness, which means the same as being full of suffering, is made into a principle. Christians are by no means strangers to the experience of nothingness. It is also an integral part of the Christian experience. The famous Jesuit theologian Francis Suarez is said to have answered the question as to what is the most necessary thing for a man to know in this way: that he should realize the absolute nothingness of the world. The experience of the nothingness of one's own being and the world is the necessary condition for the ascent of the Christian to God. As it says in the Collect for the feast of St. Sylvester on November 26, God in his mercy called the saint to a life of solitude when he was contemplating the nothingness of the world beside an open grave.

In both the Old and the New Testaments man is continually reminded of his nothingness. In Psalm 38 (39), 4 we read:

> Lord, let me know my end and what is the measure of my
>   days;
> let me know how fleeting my life is!
> Behold, thou hast made my days a few handbreadths,
> and my lifetime is nothing in thy sight.
> Surely every man stands as a mere breath.
> Surely man goes about as a shadow!

[10] Cf. Georg Siegmund, *Sein oder Nichtsein. Die Frage des Selbstmordes* (Trier, 1961), pp. 192ff.

Surely for nought are they in turmoil;
man heaps up and knows not who will gather!

In Isaiah 40, 17 it is said:

All the nations are as nothing before him;
they are accounted by him as less than nothing and empti-
ness.

It is God who

brings princes to nought,
and makes the rulers of the earth as nothing. (Is. 40, 23)

And to the gods it is said:

Behold, you are nothing
and your work is nought;
an abomination is he who chooses you. (Is. 41, 24)

In his letter to the Galatians Paul castigates those who pride
themselves on being *something,* pointing out that they are deceiving themselves, for in fact they are *nothing:* "For if anyone
thinks he is something, when he is nothing, he is deceiving himself" (Gal. 6, 3). We should not therefore seek for empty fame,
or compete with each other or envy each other.

Paul stresses repeatedly that the desire for fame is idle because
man has *nothing of himself,* nothing that he has not received
(1 Cor. 4, 7). He says with Jeremiah: "Let him who boasts boast
of the Lord" (2 Cor. 10, 17). Paul blames man's feverish desire to *make* something of himself in order to *be* something of
himself. The mystics, like Paul, have seen it as fundamental to
Christianity that the world and man in essence are nothing and
the desire to make something of himself is the express contradiction of true faith in God.

Let us mention here that the thought of Kierkegaard, Sartre
and others, as well as the experience of modern writers, has

given us the means to analyze phenomenologically and psycho-
logically the feverish desire of man to "found" his own "existence" on his own actions, and to confirm the truth of Paul's
position.

Paul wants to unmask a particular form of self-deception.
Man should know that he has nothing of himself and even that
which he has gained by his own efforts he has only gained with
the help of what he already possessed, which was pure "gift".
And his effort itself is not entirely his own doing, for it is not of
himself that his will or his intelligence gives him the means to
do it. The man who does not have this self-knowledge but im-
agines that he can ascribe his action and his being to himself
is deluded by his own pride. A foolish desire to be his own
keeps him from knowledge of the simple fact that no man can
be his own in the sense of giving himself what he possesses.

Kierkegaard has described the vain attempt—which is a fight
against reality—to be eternal of oneself. The attempt ends in
the "despair of him who wants to be eternal of himself".[11]

A similar resignation and dumb despair is the chief characteristic of a man who consciously or unconsciously has Buddhist
tendencies. The cultured Japanese thinks it proper to have a
"tragic" expression. He likes resignation. *Schkata ga nai* ("What
does it matter?") is a household word in Japan. There is no use
worrying; one should simply take what comes. It is thought to
be a sign of greatness not to be content with life, to withdraw
from it with an expression which is always sad. It is sadness at
"existence", and yet to endure this sadness is a "heroic" pose
which many like to adopt. A permanent resentment against
existence becomes part of the character. There is no more
humor, no liberating laughter, at most a wry smile.

A significant Japanese word is *akirame*. This word is probably
most appropriately translated "resignation" or "surrender" in
modern poetry and religious writing. "The modern usage of
this word expresses *Weltschmerz* or sadness at existence—hu-

[11] Soren Kierkegaard, *Die Krankheit zum Tode* (ed. H. Diem and
W. Rest) (Cologne, 1956), pp. 99ff.

man existence in particular—in a hostile world. The Buddhist interpretation relates this word with *akiraka ni miru*—that is, to see clearly, to see or apprehend the absolute through the dark veil of this world, which can only happen when instincts and inclinations are renounced. The original meaning of *akirame* appears to have been that man gives himself up, renounces his personal wishes in order not to conflict with the wishes of a superior. The word's triple etymology makes it hardly surprising that it is used so often." [12]

Resignation includes the silent renunciation of any absolute or personal meaning to life. Personal consciousness then becomes a burden, a disvalue, which one would like to be rid off and return to the unconsciousness of plant life. This burden can only be taken away by faith in a personal creator, the God and giver of meaning. As evidence we could quote the prayer from a diary of a Japanese girl student:

"God of glory, when my reason which you created did not yet know you and my will was not yet directed toward you, when I did not yet know that everything in the universe silently tends toward the highest goal of existence, I was overcome with the thought of my own meaninglessness and I longed to return to the unconsciousness of the world of nature. I was at pains to know what purposes I and the things around me could fulfill, and this longing became excessive. As consciousness was suffering to me, I wished to return to the unconscious world where I saw natural things silently obeying marvelous laws. When I began to value my consciousness as a unique good, this was because I understood that I had received it from you, O personal God. When I began to follow the narrow way to the deepest reality, my mind was satisfied with the knowledge of you, and my will was satisfied by my striving toward you. My consciousness was reunited with you, its source, and your creature returned to you, the personal God." [13]

[12] M. Heinrichs, *Katholische Theologie und asiatisches Denken* (Mainz, 1963), p. 50.

[13] Heinrich Dumoulin, *Ostliche Meditation und christliche Mystik* (Freiburg/Munich, 1966), p. 166.

While her blistering resignation lasted, her "consciousness" gave her nothing but pain; it was an unendurable burden and she wanted to be released from it and to return to the unconsciousness of inanimate things. When she realized that this consciousness was a good which she had received, she was forced to ask who had given it to her; then she began to value it positively and sought to return to the ground of her being. This search cannot end with an apersonal absolute but must lead to a being with that absolute self-possession human beings so sorely feel the lack of.

This is not the Buddhist way of salvation. The Buddhist way of meditation does not seek reunion with the personal ground of existence, but to be released from consciousness and united with the immanent (and impersonal) ground of being.

If we seek for the principles of Eastern spirituality and to compare them with the Western, we pass through levels of difference to the common basis, the *anima naturaliter Christiana* whose inmost desire is for the eternal.

That human nature is imprinted with the absolute is true also for Buddhism. Buddhist resignation is fundamentally "disappointment". The expectation was of an absolute person. Man who is constantly changing cannot be considered as this person. A true person would be in absolute and permanent possession of himself and in no danger of disintegration. He would be capable of maintaining the highest level of feeling. This expectation contains an *a priori* knowledge of the absolute; otherwise it would not be disappointed. In the depths of the human soul lies the desire for a being which is unconditional and in full self-possession. This is the measure by which actual human being is measured and found wanting. Actual human being is accounted nothingness because it is not like God. The statement that man is not a person is a demand for a person like God. The empirical "I" is not allowed to count because the eternal Self, the Atman is desired. Union with it is true salvation, or at least it would be true salvation if it were attainable.

Or we could put it all in another way. If one longs for something, one feels empty because of the lack of it and longs to possess it. Even when we do not have what we long for, we have a certain knowledge of it. We can say something about what it should be like to satisfy certain conditions in ourselves which we do know about. We can do a sort of transcendental analysis and describe what it would have to be like in order to satisfy our need.

In my *Psychologie des Gottesglaubens* I have tried to do this transcendental analysis in the chapter "Unruhe zu Gott" (Restlessness for God).[14] This restlessness is common to all men, even those who call themselves unbelievers. In spite of skepticism which bars the way to God, in spite of false notions of God, in spite of every denial of God and every proclamation of his "death", modern man still craves for the absolute. This is also true of Buddhists. The analysis of this restlessness is what must be the basis of any real dialogue with non-Christians.

[14] Georg Siegmund, *Psychologie des Gottesglaubens*, (Münster-Schwarzach, ²1966), pp. 48-99.

Heinrich Dumoulin, S.J./*Oiso, Japan*

A Dialogue with Zen Buddhists

Religious dialogues were given strong endorsement by Vatican Council II, and they have increased greatly since then. The Church is now engaged in intramural dialogues, in dialogues with other Christians, in dialogues with non-Christian religions, and in dialogues with non-believers. Of the four types mentioned, the dialogue with non-Christian religions is still in its early stages. But the conciliar texts did spell out some fundamental principles,[1] and a new and controversial branch of theology—the theology of religions—has contributed valuable insights to the whole question of dialogue.[2]

[1] See the following: *Declaration on the Relationship of the Church to Non-Christian Religions, Declaration on Religious Freedom, Dogmatic Constitution on the Church* (esp. section 16).

[2] Of the extensive Catholic literature on this subject we would suggest the following: K. Rahner, "Das Christentum und die nichtchristlichen Religionen," in *Schriften zur Theologie*, V, 136-158; *idem*, "Weltgeschichte und Heilsgeschichte," *ibid.*, 115-136; H. Schlette, *Die Religionen als Thema der Theologie* (Freiburg, 1964); H. Fries, "Das Christentum und die Religionen der Welt," in *Das Christentum und die Weltreligionen*, edited by K. Forster (Würzburg, 1965), pp. 13-37; G. Thils, *Propos et problèmes de la théologie des religions non-chrétiennes* (Castermann, 1966); *idem, Syncrétisme ou Catholicité* (Castermann, 1967); H. Waldenfels, "Zum Gespräch der Christenheit mit der nichtchristlichen Welt," in *Kairos*, 1966, 8, 179-192.

The Protestant contribution to this topic has also been considerable. See, for example, P. Tillich, *Christianity and the Encounter of the World*

Dialogue itself is an eminently practical matter, and practical experience is a prime prerequisite for fruitful results. Professional theology would do well to consider the practical experience of those in mission lands. Only concrete and well-rounded knowledge of our partners in the dialogue can provide us with the proper guidelines for such an undertaking.

The present article is a rather detailed account of the first meeting between Zen Buddhists and Christians. The meeting was arranged by the Quakers under the direction of Dr. Douglas V. Steere (who was an observer at Vatican Council II), and it was held in Oiso, Japan from March 27 to April 1 of this year. Hopefully, this account of the meeting will contribute to our dialogue with other world religions. A description of how the meeting went and what topics were discussed may offer theologians some starting points for further study.

Ten Zen Buddhists were invited from each of the two Japanese schools of Zen Buddhism—the Rinzai school and the Soto school.[2a] Ten Protestants and ten Catholics were also invited. The participants discussed two major themes in five successive morning sessions, alternating the theme each day. Thus three sessions were devoted to "the interior way", and two sessions examined "man's responsibility for bringing order into the world".

Each participant addressed himself to the theme in a fifteen- or twenty-minute speech, then the floor was opened for free discussion. In the evenings, Buddhist or Christian arts were displayed, or else the morning discussion was picked up once again. Afternoons were left free for personal contact.

The open outdoors was most conducive to intimate personal

Religions (New York-London, 1965); E. Benz, *Ideen zu einer Theologie der Religionsgeschichte* (Mainz, 1960); R. Slater, *Can Christians Learn from Other Religions* (New York, 1963); St. Neill, *Christian Faith and Other Faiths* (London, 1961); C. Bleeker, *Christ in Modern Athens* (Leiden, 1965); G. Rosenkranz, *Der christliche Glaube angesichts der Weltreligionen* (Sammlung Dalp, 1966).

[2a] *Translator's note:* the Rinzai school stresses a more abrupt breakthrough to enlightenment than does the Soto school; the latter concentrates on a gradual process.

contacts. The strong emphasis on religious experiences stirred the inner depths of the spirit, and it is in these depths alone that a truly fruitful encounter can take place.

I

THE INTERIOR WAY

Detailed consideration of the interior way was meant to encourage the participants to discuss their personal religious experiences and to discover deeper and more intimate connections between them.

Christian Experiences

The Christian theologians sought to explain their faith to their Zen Buddhist brothers. They also succeeded to a large extent in bringing out points of contact with Buddhist religious practices.

The Protestant theologian, Kazo Kitamori, spoke of his conversion to Christianity, and explained how the deeply religious atmosphere in the home of his Buddhist parents contributed to this conversion. The Christian belief in God freed him from his anxious quest for the meaning of life, and the problem of sin brought him to Jesus Christ, the mediator and redeemer. Christ's cross revealed God's infinite love embodied in the pain of God. This served as the basis for his Lutheran-oriented study of grace and justification, *Theology of the Pain of God;* it is the most striking and original Japanese formulation of Christian faith to appear in our times.[3]

Sin and the cross were also the central Christian experiences for two Protestant theologians from the Free-Church Movement. Both are scripture scholars who received their training in Germany. Masao Sekine is an Old Testament specialist, Seyichi Yagi is a New Testament specialist.

[3] The work appeared in Japan soon after the end of World War II. English Translation: *Theology of the Pain of God* (Richmond, Virginia: John Knox Press, 1965). For a Catholic assessment see the review of P. Nemeshegyi in *The Japan Missionary Bulletin,* April 1967, 21: 187-190.

Sekine spoke of his conversion and interior transformation, and the theological truth which this brought home to him: that justification and sanctification were both unified in the new creation effected by Christ. His account was one of the most moving reports of the entire conference. Having experienced the impact of Christian renovation, he now finds it difficult to maintain his personal experience of Christian life on an even keel with his biblical scholarship, to which he has devoted his life. His younger colleague, Seyichi Yagi, has the same difficulty.

Protestant theologians see a connection between the Buddhist religious experience of the "non-I" and the Christian theology of the cross. The death of the self-centered ego is a work of grace achieved by Christ's death on the cross. They feel it can be compared to the abandonment of the subjective "I" that takes place in the Zen Buddhist process of enlightenment. This was brought out most clearly by Yagi when he told how he encountered Buddhism through the literature of Zen.

For Kitamori, the main religious contribution of Buddhism is the total conquest of dualism. His Lutheran theology of the cross strives to eliminate all dualism and to achieve absolute and perfect unity. He believes that Oriental thought can help Christian theology to gain a deeper appreciation of the mystery of unity in God and Christ.

The Catholic participants in the conference focused on the notion of prayer when they discussed the interior way. They tried to clarify the relationship between specifically Christian prayer and Zen meditation. The three Catholic reports on this theme agree on one point: there is no unbridgeable gap between the two types of spirituality.

The first report, made by this author, stressed the polarity and the complementarity of the two schools of prayer. The basic difference between the Oriental and the Western approach seems to be summed up in the contrast between silent meditation and dialogic prayer. But there is no sharp and clear-cut division between the two. Christian spirituality does focus on assembling before God, speaking to him, and having a personal encounter with him; but it then leads us on to silent repose, to deep stillness, and to perfect simplicity. In this latter atmosphere the divine mystery is experienced as infinite love transcending the boundaries of the individual. The mystery of God, as it is experienced on the higher levels of prayer, lies beyond words and concepts. Such experiences have helped to develop the notion of the "via negativa" in Christian spirituality. And this notion is akin to the Oriental way of negation (*Mu*—the refusal to affirm or deny).[4]

The young Japanese Carmelite, Ichiro Okumura, combines the loftier values of Japanese tradition with those of Carmelite spirituality. Soon after he had become a Christian, he became acquainted with Carmelite spirituality through the writings of St. John of the Cross and he chose this way for his own. When he entered the Carmelite order, he brought with him his familiarity with Zen discipline and his intimate knowledge of the writings of the great Zen master, Dogen. He feels deeply indebted to the prayer tradition of his order, but he also believes that Christian spirituality can be enriched by Zen meditation, because the latter appreciates the unity of body and soul in man and knows how to "pray with the body". As he sees it, full-fledged prayer must involve "the whole man—his head, his heart and his body".

On the final day H. M. Enomiya Lassalle, whose knowledge of Zen meditation is unrivalled, spelled out the relationship between Zen exercises and Christianity. He pointed out that he was led to the practice of Zen, not by any personal religious crisis or by doubts about Christianity, but by the desire to penetrate more deeply into the Japanese mentality. Zen has played a decisive role in shaping this mentality.

From his experiences with Zen practices, Enomiya Lassalle is convinced that Zen offers us the possibility of overcoming certain difficulties that he had encountered for a long time in the

[4] On the negative theology of Oriental and Western mysticism see H. Dumoulin, *Östliche Meditation und christliche Mystik* (Freiburg, 1966), pp. 98-126.

traditional prayer methods of Christianity. He was, of course, familiar with the Christian mystics; but the mystical approach in Christianity did not seem to be readily accessible.

In his first attempts at Zen meditation, by contrast, he experienced a new and undreamed of possibility for spiritual recollection and concentration. This possibility, he felt, could and should be of the utmost importance for Christian prayer. So he proceeded with Zen practices, and those familiar with Zen could well imagine how much patience and persistence it took. He put himself under the direction of a Zen master, but he confessed that he had not attained enlightenment (*kensho*). He concluded by spelling out the value of Zen exercises for Christian spirituality.[5]

Zen Buddhist Experiences

The reports made by the Zen Buddhists were not so homogeneous as those of the Christian participants; hence they cannot be categorized too easily. One set of accounts deals simply with personal religious development, depicting the growth of Buddhist piety, the deepening of the individual's spiritual and religious sense, and the nourishment of the interior life through discipline and study. Another set of accounts relates the experiences of those whose religious outlook was influenced by Zen Buddhism but has developed outside the boundaries of Buddhist institutions. Finally, the report of the Zen master, Mumon Yamada, must stand by itself. For it is the only one that depicts Zen enlightenment as actually experienced by a Zen master.

Under the first set of accounts I shall group four reports: two from members of the Rinzai school and two from members of the Soto school. On the first day we listened to the Abbot of the Rinzai cloister in Kyoto, Zenkei Shibayama, who is one of the most experienced and distinguished leaders of Zen Buddhism in

---

[5] H. Enomiya Lassalle, S.J. has spelled out his viewpoint in two books: *Zen: Weg zur Erleuchtung* (Vienna, 1960); and *Zen-Buddhismus* (Cologne, 1966).

Japan. His report was quite reserved, perhaps because it was the first day and an atmosphere of mutual trust had not yet developed. Although the Abbot spoke of his religious development, he did not bring up his personal religious experiences.

His motives for entering the path of Zen were those of any religious man: he renounced the world after recognizing the fleeting nature of worldly things and the enduring values of the spirit. Like many great religious figures, he was greatly influenced in early childhood by his pious mother. Her early death precipitated his decision to devote his life to the practice of Zen. Thus he is one of those tireless practitioners who keep moving ahead throughout their life and find rest only after their death.

The Abbot stressed his deep respect for Christianity, and in particular for its social work on behalf of the poor and needy. Unfortunately, pressing duties prevented him from staying until the end of the five-day meeting, and he was not able to contribute his valuable insights, as a Zen Buddhist, to the second topic.

The only female participant at the conference was Kachiko Yokogawa. It was D. T. Suzuki, her family's benefactor, who took an interest in this gifted child and made possible her scholarly education. It was he who introduced her to the deep riches of Buddhism. She recounted her religious life in the Rinzai school of Zen Buddhism and told how her participation in long periods of intensive meditation (*sesshin*) enabled her to acquire a deeper understanding of Zen.

The two representatives of the Soto school belong to the faculty of Komazawa University in Tokyo. Reirin Yamada is the President, and Yasuaki Nara is a specialist in the primary languages of Buddhism (Pali and Sanskrit). Nara's encounter with foreigners and their earnest questions about Zen stimulated him to acquire a deeper understanding of, and familiarity with, the teachings and practices of the Soto school. He came to see the central importance of actual practice, for it is only through this that one can bridge the chasm between doctrine and actual life. Zen is essentially a way of life, not a body of doctrine; it is the life style of Buddha incorporated into one's everyday behavior. The spirit of the Soto school, which does not strive for sudden enlightenment or abrupt encounters, looks with reserve on the state of ultimate enlightenment (*satori*). The guiding norm in Soto Zen, as laid down by its founder, Dogen, is enlightened living from day to day.

The report of Reirin Yamada, a university president and a master of Soto Zen, depicted this ideal of enlightened everyday living. Here was a man whose job kept him busy from morning to night. Problems, vexations, difficulties and annoyances were part and parcel of his work. The only thing that could bring free-dom and tranquillity to his burdened spirit was a steady diet of Zen meditation, in which he could breathe the air of enlighten-ment and of nature. The cosmic experience of entering into unity with all things somehow forestalls death and confers a feeling of deep inner security, like that of the infant in his mother's womb. Man finds harmony and nothing can unnerve him. When he en-counters hardships, he returns to breathe this atmosphere once again. Zen meditation, carried out in the daily conduct of life, is the solution to all difficulties.

Professor Masao Abe is not a Buddhist monk, but his study of religion brought him to Zen Buddhism. His whole life has been marked by an earnest and unselfish quest for truth. Being of a deeply religious nature, he was unable to find satisfaction in a secular vocation. He returned to the university to pursue philo-sophical and religious studies exclusively. At Kyoto University Professor Shinichi Hisamatsu became his teacher in scholarly study and in the art of living. At this point his religious develop-ment came to a turning point, and he embraced Zen Buddhism.

As a young man, he was brought up in the faith of the Amida Buddha. He had earnestly sought salvation in the practice of uttering the Buddha's holy name (*Nembutsu*). This particular practice, which relies on "the power of another" (*tariki*), is con-sidered to be the "easy way" in Japanese religious annals. But Professor Abe came to realize that it is very difficult to practice real Nembutsu, for mere vocal utterances do not accomplish anything. Nor is personal effort enough. Authentic Nembutsu requires that one assume the Amida Buddha's salvific intention (*hongan*) to save all living things. This Nembutsu proceeds from Buddha and penetrates the believer's mouth and body; in this way all duality is taken away, and the believer attains salvation and life.

Quite obviously, this conception of *Nembutsu* is akin to the position of Zen Buddhism. The groping pupil found that the personality of his new-found professor (Hisamatsu) cast doubts on Nembutsu. The way of Zen, exemplified by his new Master, went beyond Nembutsu and led to the ultimate conquest of all duality. It brought one to absolute, creative freedom.

Professor Abe described the Zen conception of unity with great clarity. But his own religious quest does not seem to have come to an end as yet. His search and his questioning continues, as he himself made clear in the ensuing discussion. He is deeply interested in what he calls the "original roots of Buddhism". By this he does not mean the historical beginnings of Buddhism, but the original essence of the way marked out by Buddha. At the same time he is engaged in a real dialogue with Christianity. For many years he has given much thought to the notion of grace and salvation through a higher power.

Professor Torataro Shimomura was the most representative delegate from the Kyoto School, the only distinctively Japanese school of philosophy. This original school of thought owes much to Zen.[6] Professor Shimomura is a philosopher and a first-generation disciple of the school's founders—Kitaro Nishida and Hajime Tanabe. Shimomura does not regard himself as a religious adherent to Buddhism, as he pointed out at the beginning of his report. Like so many of his countrymen, particularly its intel-

[6] On the relationship of the Kyoto school of philosophy to the metaphysics of Zen Buddhism see H. Waldenfels, "Absolute Nothingness: Preliminary Considerations on a Central Notion in the Philosophy of K. Nishida and the Kyoto School," in *Monumenta Nipponica*, Sophia University, Tokyo, 1966, 21: 354-391.

lectuals, he does not profess any religious belief and skirts the precincts of religion. Unlike many others, however, he does not look on religion with indifference and he is quick to admit this. He has had close contacts with Buddhism (as a student) and with Christianity (as a teacher), but he has never joined a formal religious community. If one were to ask him what his relationship to Buddhism was, he would not be able to say definitely whether he was a Buddhist or not. Such an attitude is quite sensible in a Buddhist frame of reference, because the concept "Buddhist" has no sharp and clear definition.

Shimomura regards this as one of the important differences between Buddhism and Christianity, or between Oriental and Western religions in general. In Western Christianity, doctrine, theology and concepts play a dominant role; in Japan, religion represents one's way of life. In the discussion that followed, Shimomura elaborated on his reservations about Christianity. They deserve serious attention because they are shared by many Japanese intellectuals. One of his major complaints against Christianity is its antagonistic attitude toward other religions. This has led to religious wars in the West, and Christianity's attempts to absorb the religious and cultural traditions of Oriental countries.

The Zen Master, Mumon Yamada, gave the final report at the last morning session. Throughout the conference period he had many worthwhile things to say in the discussion periods and in private colloquies. In his report, he talked simply of his early childhood and his student days. He spoke of his contacts with Confucian wisdom and with Christianity, and of his high ideals. His decision to renounce the world was based on the Bodhisattva ideal of Mahayana Buddhism, summed up in these words: "To renounce oneself and serve mankind." Yamada readily acknowledged the close resemblance between the Bodhisattva ideal and the Christ ideal.

Yamada's noble resolve led him into a dark night of the soul. Because of illness he had to leave the strict Buddhist cloister that he had entered. Back at home he endured months of bodily pain, deep loneliness and total abandonment. One spring day he dragged himself to the veranda of his parents' house. A gentle wind played over his head. He thought to himself: "What is the wind? What is the air? Am I really alone? Isn't the wind and the air always around me?" Deep inside he felt himself sustained by an ever present and sublime force. Bolstered by this conviction, he found the strength to devote himself to Zen exercises once again. This time around, he used the health techniques prescribed and followed by the well known Zen Master, Hakuin,[7] and thus regained his health. He continued to pursue authentic Zen meditation until he suddenly woke to full enlightenment while gazing at the brilliant red color of the maple leaves.

Master Mumon described enlightenment as the moment of total self-forgetfulness, of seeing without seeing and knowing without knowing, in which being is born out of nothingness. The person who has attained enlightenment is truly a human being. He is no longer male or female, young or old. He is just a human being, at total oneness with reality, fully happy and free.

Master Mumon explained the activity of an enlightened person in terms of the four-part Rinzai formula. The enlightened one acts (1) subjectively (interiorly) and not objectively (exteriorly); (2) exteriorly and not interiorly; (3) exteriorly and interiorly; (4) neither interiorly nor exteriorly. Exteriorly everything is one; interiorly the enlightened one is free.

One comment of Master Mumon might surprise us. But it is a typical remark and it deserves our attention. He spoke several times of his sympathetic affinities to Christianity, of his respect for the Bible in particular. But prayer involving the use of words, such as that to be found in Christian piety, seems totally unsatisfactory to him. Dialogic prayer is completely alien to this master of Zen, whose eyes are focused inward completely.

[7] Hakuin describes the health techniques used by Master Mumon (deep breathing and the so-called "butter method") in his work, *Yasen Kanna:* English translation by R. Shaw and W. Schiffer in *Monumenta Nipponica*, Tokyo, 1957, 101-127.

II

Responsibility in the World

The other theme of the conference complemented the first and brought us into contact with the needs and crises of the present day. It was in the discussion periods that the real issues were brought out. However, despite the lengthy discussions, certain things were never fully clarified. Considering the complexity of the issues, this was not surprising.

Here I should like to summarize the main points expressed at the conference. They can be classified under three headings: (1) the relationship between one's religious outlook and the call to serve society; (2) man's responsibilities in shaping new social structures today; (3) specific social issues—in particular, the problem of world peace.

Religion and Social Service

During the discussions, considerable differences in motivation and emphasis were evident on specific issues. Yet the participants seemed to be in agreement on one basic point: man has a religious responsibility to bring order into society. The Japanese formulation of the theme was something less than precise; as a result, some of the participants viewed the theme too narrowly, interpreting it to mean charitable activities.

The first speaker, for example, seemed to interpret it thus. He was Professor Shōkin Furuta, an historian and a disciple of D. T. Suzuki from the Rinzai school. He stated that Buddhism, and Zen Buddhism in particular, has no direct mission to engage in social works. As a cultural force, Buddhism has played an important role in Japanese history (e.g., Kōbō Daishi), but social activity is not its immediate task; the great reformers, Dogen and Shinran, made this clear. The work of religion lies totally within the religious sphere.

In terms of Zen Buddhism, everything is aimed at renouncing the world and the ego and acquiring the perspective achieved in enlightenment. Here Furuta quoted the ancient Japanese saying: "Go into the mountain and then come out of the mountain."

This expression was to crop up many times during the discussions. Everyone agreed that no one could render genuine religious service to mankind and society if he did not experience the solitary atmosphere of the mountain; in other words, he has to die to the world both internally and externally. Going into the mountain and returning from it is equivalent to the Christian ideal of combining contemplation with activity in the world. To do both is not easy, as many speakers pointed out.

Mumon Yamada deplored the fact that today many Buddhists lack a real sense of social responsibility. They are quite willing to go off to the mountain, but they do not return to serve society. The person who has attained authentic enlightenment comes back to serve society.

Time and again the Zen Buddhists (e.g., Eshin Nishimura and Takashi Hirata of the Rinzai school) stressed the transcendent value of ultimate enlightenment (*satori*) and the priority of inner fulfillment over external activity. This naturally raised a question: What is the essential relationship between the quest for enlightenment and service to one's fellow men? At the height of the discussion Dr. Steere formulated the question for Christians, but it applied equally well for the Zen Buddhists. He put it this way: "Is responsibility for one's fellow man and for society part of the essence of the Christian experience?"

Apropos of Christianity, the answer seemed obvious to everyone; so the discussion focused on Zen Buddhism. Mumon Yamada was asked to explain the Buddhist position and he discussed it in great detail. He also brought up the story of St. Francis Assisi's meeting with the leper, which Dr. Steere had used to exemplify the Christian notion of finding God in others. Yamada was quick to admit that it was a splendid example of enlightenment; but he asserted that it was Francis' embrace, not his alms, that saved the leper. Gold and gifts are the least important elements. The enlightened person offers himself and all reality.

What does all this mean in Zen terms? During the conference Mumon Yamada explained the meaning on several different occasions. Enlightenment overcomes all duality, eliminates the barrier between oneself and others, and establishes unity. The enlightened person discovers full unity and is at one with other beings. The other person is myself, as is the mountain and the flower. And since there is no separation between the self and others, service to one's fellow men is a foregone conclusion for the enlightened person.

Now when service to one's fellow man is based on this principle—the unity of all things as experienced in enlightenment—this does not rule out the personal worth of the individual or his neighbor. But this worth is set within the more general framework of cosmic order. It would seem that the basic Buddhist virtue of compassion (*jihi*), taught by Buddha himself, provides a more realistic foundation for service to society. This virtue was mentioned often at the conference and was highly valued by all the Buddhists present; yet its significance for the whole question of social service was not brought out.

Reforming Social Structures

The second theme also raised the whole complex of questions concerning religion's role in the development of new social structures. Our technological era requires such new structures; without them the development of man's spirit will be seriously undermined.

This sentiment cropped up frequently, even in a letter sent by Professor Shinichi Hisamatsu. He is the acknowledged leader of the scholarly and intellectual faction of the Rinzai school, but illness forced him to stay away from the conference. In his letter Professor Hisamatsu noted the twofold crisis of the present day, caused by secularization and man's alienation. However, the whole problem was the subject of hints and allusions during the conference, rather than of explicit and detailed treatment.

Professor Tetsutaro Ariga is a Protestant theologian who is interested in the history of religions. He spoke of the created order, in which God has chosen that human history be played out. This order is good because it has been created by God, but it puts a duty on man. Pursuing the same line of thought, Professor Yukio Irie (a Japanese Quaker and an able panel moderator) stressed man's historicity. Throughout his life man is called to adapt to changing times, to follow God's direction and cooperate in actualizing God's plan for the world.

The young Japanese Dominican, Shigeto Oshida, made an urgent appeal for religion's involvement in social service; without such involvement religion would not be capable of winning man's adherence. But he also went on to spell out his vision of a new world and a new social order, to be built through the combined efforts of all men of goodwill. Today's young people cannot be enlisted in purely charitable activities; they are looking for a total picture. Only a new and comprehensive program for a better world, rooted in religious principles, can galvanize their energies. This appeal made a deep impression on all, particularly on the young Zen Buddhists who were obviously moved.

The reports of two Zen Buddhists, Eshin Nishimura and Takashi Hirata, offered valuable take-off points for deeper consideration of contemporary social problems. They stressed the fundamental historicity of human existence. Eshin Nishimura emphasized that historical specificity was an essential factor in man's life. He felt that critical examination of history and man's historical milieu was a major task today and would enhance man's freedom. Takashi Hirata discussed the dynamic thrust of existence in history. To fulfill his vocation in a constantly changing world, man must live the present historical moment. Thus religion must constantly adapt to changing circumstances in order to serve mankind.

Unfortunately, the various take-off points were never really tied together. The Christian ideal looks toward the future, while the Zen Buddhist ideal tries to grasp the present moment. No attempt was made to tie these two ideals together, but such an attempt might have produced a more fruitful discussion.

World Peace

One specific issue brought up was religion's role in the preservation of world peace. Junichi Asano (a Protestant theologian

and scripture scholar, deeply involved in social action) stressed
the urgency of this issue and called upon the conference to take
a stand on war—the Vietnam war in particular. This request was
directed to the Christian participants because the Vietnam war
is unanimously condemned by Japanese Buddhists.

Dr. Steere took it upon himself to clarify this issue, spelling
out the pacifist position of the Quakers (which is quite well
known). He noted that the Protestant Churches of America and
the World Council of Churches had also taken a stand against
America's conduct of the war in Vietnam. Moreover, Pope Paul
VI's urgent pleas for peace indicated that the top leadership in
the Catholic Church was totally committed to the quest for peace.

The discussion period was running long, so the participants
let Dr. Steere's remarks suffice. They did not want to enter a detailed discussion of political issues, and they were in agreement
on their positive desire for world peace.

III

The Conference in Retrospect

The meeting in Oiso was the first full-scale inter-religious dialogue to take place in Japan. It was a friendly and fruitful meeting that came off well. This was due, in no small measure, to the
fact that the conference was well organized. The participants
were well chosen and their number was kept within reasonable
limits.

Zen Buddhists are a compact and highly trained group. Since
the end of World War II, Zen has had a great impact on the
West. Its representatives have exchanged ideas with Western intellectuals, and hence are especially well prepared for East-West
dialogues. More recently intramural dialogues have increased between Christians through the growth of the ecumenical movement. Thus, on both sides, there was great readiness to engage
in dialogue, to display mutual respect and mutual trust, to listen
to and learn from one another.

What a given individual learned at the conference depended on his own particular interests and openness. Indeed it is possible that some participants, as individuals, may have learned more from the conference than his group did. However, each side did learn from the other. The Buddhists, for example, were impressed by the social awareness of Christians; they were motivated to intensify their efforts in that direction. The Christians, on the other hand, were given an up-to-date lesson in the proper hierarchy of religious values. They were taught that openness to the world must never be pursued at the expense of interior contemplation. The priority of the interior life, as exemplified by the religious men of Asia, must never be challenged.

The sense of religious community was cultivated during the conference by appropriate get-togethers. Mumon Yamada celebrated the tea ceremony twice, and it was an unforgettable experience. The revered old man was dressed in a coarse woolen garment, quite different from his silk robes (abbot's garb). Silent and totally absorbed, he prepared the tea; yet he was alert to every gesture and had a wondrous smile for everyone there. The harmonious balance of his personality is a rare thing even among Zen masters, for he combines deep interior spirituality with keen intelligence and gracious charm. His presence did much to cement the feeling of religious community.

Many participants availed themselves of the opportunity to frequent the religious ceremonies of other groups. They readily joined in concelebrated Catholic Masses, silent Quaker meetings, and periods of Zen meditation.

The Common Ground

Throughout the conference, references were made to John XXIII's words about "the common ground on which all religions rest". In his closing address Abbot Zenkei Shibayama spoke movingly of his experience of the common element in all religions, and of religion's commitment to community. This prepared the way for a discussion of the "common ground" on the next-to-last evening.

Many participants hoped to see some formula adopted on this point. They looked for some philosophical formulation in which the Kyoto school approximates the outlook of Western philosophy. But this discussion soon came to a dead end. The common element, real though it may be, cannot be crystallized in words. Dialogue requires that religions recognize and acknowledge their differences.

This does not contradict the claim of absolute truth that is part and parcel of Christianity. Other religions, too, cherish some notion of absolute conviction. As the Buddhists pointed out, this is essential to any authentic religious outlook.

Now in the Christian religion, the notions of universality and absolute truth are grounded in the Christ event, which is not accepted by non-Christians of course. Thus the incorporation of others into Christ, however valid and basic it may be in theological terms, is not a usable concept in inter-religious dialogues.

If the Christian tries to show that non-Christian religions are in fact Christian, that his non-Christian partner in the dialogue is actually a Christian in disguise, he will encounter misunderstanding and resentment. Religious Orientals—Hindus and Buddhists in particular—find nothing more intolerable than Christianity's attempt to absorb other religions. And, as the Buddhists made clear at the conference, this seems to be the typical Christian attitude.

In inter-religious dialogue, the Christian must respect the "otherness" of his partner in the dialogue. He cannot come to such meetings with the aim of convincing or converting the non-Christian. Nor can he seek to syncretize the differences and amalgamate them into some higher unity.

How then do we approach such dialogues? We talk with each other, realizing full well that we share a common ground. We strive to gain deeper mutual understanding, deeper mutual respect and deeper empathy. We try to learn from each other and, wherever possible, to work together for the good of the human race.

This was the aim and the approach of the Oiso conference. The exchange of viewpoints enabled us to experience the true meaning of mutual understanding. The conviction that we share a common ground is an important element; but so is our respect for the fact of plurality.

BIOGRAPHICAL NOTES

JEAN-YVES JOLIF, O.P.: Born in 1923 at Rennes, France, he was ordained in 1949. He studied under the Dominicans in Lyons, at the Saulchoir, and in Paris, gaining his degrees in philosophy and theology. He is head of the philosophy course at the Catholic College in Lyons. Among his works are *Comprendre l'homme* (Paris, 1967) and "Le monde. Remarques sur la signification du terme," in *Lumière et Vie* 14 (1965), No. 74.

HENRI-MARIE FÉRET, O.P.: Born in 1904 at Vannes, France, he was ordained in 1928. He studied at the Saulchoir and the Sorbonne, receiving a doctorate in theology in 1930. He is professor of biblical catechetics at the Catholic Institute in Paris and prior of the Dominican House at Dijon. Among his published works are *Connaissance biblique de Dieu* (1955), *L'Apocalypse* (Paris, 1943) and *Pour une Église des béatitudes de la pauvreté* (1965). He writes for *Parole et Mission* and *La Vie Spirituelle*.

HANS URS VON BALTHASAR: Born in 1905 in Lucerne, Switzerland, he studied Germanic languages and philosophy in Zurich, earning a doctorate for his study of "The Eschatalogical Problem in German Literature". Many of his works have been translated into English, including *St. Thérèse of Lisieux* (1953), *Elizabeth of Dijon* (1956), *Prayer* (1961), *Theology of History* and *Martin Buber and Christianity*.

PETER STEINFELS: Born in 1941 in Chicago, he studied at the universities of Loyola in Chicago and Columbia, New York. He gained his M.A. in 1964 and is presently studying for his degree in philosophy. He is both an historian and a journalist, and is associate-editor of *Commonweal*.

FRANÇOIS LEPARGNEUR, O.P.: Born in 1925 in Paris, he was ordained in 1955. He studied at the universities of Caen, Paris, and Cornell, New York. He received his doctorates in law in 1951 and in theology in 1957. He has been professor of ecclesiology at the Dominican House of Studies in Brazil since 1959. He is presently studying for his doctorate in philosophy. He has collaborated with G. Perez and A. Gregory in *Le Problème Sacerdotal au Brésil* (Bogotá, 1965).

MARTIN EKWA, S.J.: Born in 1926 in the Congo, he was ordained in 1958. He studied at the St. Peter Canisius Institute at Kimwenza in the Congo, and at Louvain, gaining his degree in theology. He has been president of the National Bureau of Catholic Teachers in the Congo since 1960. Among his publications are *Le Congo et l'Education* (1965) and *L'Education Chrétienne au service de la Nation Congolaise* (1967).

PAUL-MARCEL LEMAIRE, O.P.: Born in 1928 in Canada, he was ordained in 1954. After studying with the Dominicans in Ottawa and at the Catholic Institute in Paris, he gained his degree in theology at the Institute of Pastoral Catechetics. Since 1964 he has been professor of theology and religious education at Montreal University. He is co-author of *L'Art et les Hommes* (Ottawa, 1967).

WILLIAM HAMILTON: A Protestant, he was born in 1924 at Evanston, Illinois. He studied at the Union Theological Seminary at Princeton University and at the University of St. Andrew. He received degrees in the arts and theology and a doctorate in philosophy (1953). He has been professor of religion at Rochester University, New York, since 1955, and is also a member of the Society for Religion in Higher Education, of the American Theological Society, and of Biblical Theologians. He has appeared on television for the National Council of Churches. Among his published works are *Radical Theology and the Death of God* (New York, 1966) with Thomas J. J. Altizer, and *The New Essence of Christianity* (New York, 1966).

JOHN EDWARD CROUZET, O.S.B.: Born in London in 1937, he was ordained in 1964. He studied at Cambridge University and Fribourg, gaining his degrees in the arts and theology; at present he lectures in dogmatic theology at Downside Abbey.

STANISLAW NAPIÓRKOWSKI, O.F.M. Conv.: Born in 1933 in Poland, he studied at the University of Lublin, receiving his doctorate in theology in 1965, and has been professor of dogmatic theology at the Catholic University of Lublin since 1964.

GEORG SIEGMUND: Born in 1903 in Austria, he was ordained in 1928. He received doctorates in philosophy in 1927 and in theology in 1934, and is professor at the College of Philosophy and Theology at Fulda in Germany. He is the author of *Psychologie des Gottesglaubens* (1966) and *Naturordnung als Quelle des Gotteserkenntnis* (1966).

HEINRICH DUMOULIN, S.J.: Born in 1905 in Germany, he was ordained in 1933. He studied at the Jesuit House of Studies in the Netherlands and at Vals, in France, gaining his doctorates in philosophy and literature, as well as a degree in theology, in Japan. He has been professor of philosophy and of the history of religions at Sophia University in Tokyo since 1941, and is secretary to the Commission of Dialogue with Non-Christian Religions in Japan. Among his published works are *Zen, Geschichte und Gestalte* (Bern 1959) and *Oestliche Meditation und christliche Mystik* (Freiburg, 1966).

International Publishers of CONCILIUM

ENGLISH EDITION
Paulist Press
Glen Rock, N. J., U.S.A.

Burns & Oates Ltd.
25 Ashley Place
London, S.W.1

DUTCH EDITION
Uitgeverij Paul Brand, N. V.
Hilversum, Netherlands

FRENCH EDITION
Maison Mame
Tours/Paris, France

JAPANESE EDITION (PARTIAL)
Nansôsha
Tokyo, Japan

GERMAN EDITION
Verlagsanstalt Benziger & Co., A.G.
Einsiedeln, Switzerland

Matthias Grunewald-Verlag
Mainz, W. Germany

SPANISH EDITION
Ediciones Guadarrama
Madrid, Spain

PORTUGUESE EDITION
Livraria Morais Editora, Ltda.
Lisbon, Portugal

ITALIAN EDITION
Editrice Queriniana
Brescia, Italy